Touched by Fire

Also by Pandit Rajmani Tigunait, Ph.D.

books

Lighting the Flame of Compassion
Inner Quest: Yoga's Answers to Life's Questions
The Himalayan Masters: A Living Tradition
Why We Fight: Practices for Lasting Peace
At the Eleventh Hour: The Biography of Swami Rama
Swami Rama of the Himalayas: His Life and Mission
Shakti: The Power in Tantra
Tantra Unveiled
From Death to Birth: Understanding Karma and Reincarnation
The Power of Mantra and the Mystery of Initiation
Shakti Sadhana: Steps to Samadhi
Seven Systems of Indian Philosophy

audio & video

Sacred Link™ Freedom from Fear Conference
   The Quest for Freedom and the Sacred Link™
   Sacred Link™ in Practice: Panel Discussion and Closing Remarks
The Spirit of the Vedas
The Spirit of the Upanishads
Pulsation of the Maha Kumbha Mela
In the Footsteps of the Sages
Living Tantra™ Series
   Tantric Traditions and Techniques
   The Secret of Tantric Rituals
   Forbidden Tantra
   Tantra and Kundalini
   Sri Chakra: The Highest Tantric Practice
   Sri Vidya: The Embodiment of Tantra
Nine Steps to Disarming the Mind

Touched by Fire

The Ongoing Journey
of a Spiritual Seeker

PANDIT RAJMANI TIGUNAIT, PH.D.

HIMALAYAN INSTITUTE®

PRESS

HONESDALE, PENNSYLVANIA, USA

Himalayan Institute Press
952 Bethany Turnpike
Honesdale, PA 18431

www.HimalayanInstitute.org

Printed in China

The paper used in this publication meets the minimum requirements
of American National Standard for Information Sciences—Permanence
of Paper for Printed Library Materials, ANSI Z39.48-1984.

Library of Congress Cataloging-in-Publication Data

Tigunait, Rajmani, 1953-
    Touched by fire : the ongoing journey of a spiritual seeker /
    Pandit Rajmani Tigunait.
        p. cm.
    ISBN-13: 978-0-8938-9239-5
    ISBN-10: 0-89389-239-4 (pbk. : alk. paper)
    1. Tigunait, Rajmani, 1953– 2. Spiritual biography—India.
    3. Hindus—India—Biography. I. Title.

BL1175.T483A3 2005
294.5'092—dc22   2004028449

Table *of* Contents

chapter one
A Child *of* Two Worlds

chapter two
I Find My Way

chapter three
Living *with* Grace

chapter four
Miracles *and* Mysticism

chapter five
The Way *of* Providence

chapter six

Tantric Masters

chapter seven

Touched *by* Fire

chapter eight

The Flame *in the* Cave

To Thee who made me wonder forever:
Life, if thou art so mysterious,
then what a mystery thy master must be.

Foreword

This book is a remarkable portrayal of the sculpturing of a spiritual teacher. In it, you will see rare glimpses of the invisible hands of the Divine as they mold a spiritual master, the man we know today as Pandit Rajmani Tigunait. Fortunate are those who know they are meeting a true master, either personally or in the pages of a book. Encounters with such people do not happen without divine grace. This I know from my own personal experience.

I write this preface with reverence for Panditji and with deep humility, for I myself am far from sacred learning and spiritual wisdom. But as I read these pages, I found myself identifying with the happenings recounted here, many of which are almost too incredible to be believed. Seeing can be the beginning of believing. At the very least this book will introduce you to a living sage who is readily accessible and with whom you can communicate—one who lives divinity in all its aspects, one who has been sculptured by spiritual immortals.

Here is just a sampling of this divine sculpturing: Panditji was born into a family of royal teachers. As a young boy he would often sneak into his father's private room to read the scriptures. His instincts and inclinations led him to Sanskrit school, which he reached the first time by crossing a flood-swollen, snake-ridden canal. What took others months and years to learn took him only days. Thrown in a compost pit six times by his uncles who wanted to acquire family land, the boy had his first physical experience of the presence of the Divine.

He enrolled in a famous university, but his rural background made him a misfit. In his final undergraduate year, he realized his parents were unable to provide for his higher education, and so he began walking upstream along the bank of the Ganga in search of divine guidance. On the way he met a great saint, who blessed him and told him, "Your job is to continue walking. When you really get exhausted, then simply stop and wait, and remember that He will pick you up."

This saint told him to go visit his parents. When he arrived at their village home, his family was being visited by their long-lost and very wealthy friends. These friends insisted on taking the young man back to the university (they lived in the same city and had arrived in their personal car—in those days very few owned one) and being a family to him while he studied for his graduate degree.

It is through this family that, a few years later, Pandit Rajmani walked into an unfamiliar building in Delhi, got into an elevator, and landed on the floor where his supreme spiritual master, Swami Rama, a sage of the Himalayas was waiting for him. On seeing Panditji, Swami Rama said, "I have been waiting for you. When are you coming to the States?" Months later, Panditji asked Swamiji, "How did I come to that hotel? Did you know that I was coming? Was it a coincidence?" Swamiji replied in two sentences: "The way of Providence is mysterious—nothing is accidental. Haven't you heard that the teacher appears when the student is prepared?"

These are only a few brief examples. The entire book is a gold mine of spiritual history to be read and contemplated again and again. The more we swim in the waves of spiritual waters, the more we realize how little we know. As we dive deeper, more is revealed to us. And then we realize how short one lifetime is to experience the ocean of it all. Pandit Rajmani Tigunait is a custodian of the lineage of sages—and he himself is an immeasurable spiritual treasure. And we, the fortunate ones, are in a position to read, and meet, him today. Remember—nothing is accidental!

In surrender,
Kiran Bedi, Ph.D.
United Nations Civilian Police Advisor
and
Magsaysay Laurete

CHAPTER ONE

A Child
of Two Worlds

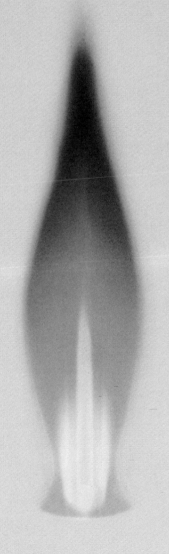

My Motherland

India is a country of extremes and contrasts. Diversity defines this land—the best of the best and the worst of the worst in human values and achievements exist here side by side. Claiming equal rights, Mercedes and bullock carts share the same road. At times, apples imported from the West flood markets in the city but onions are scarce, even while millions of tons rot in the villages for lack of transport. Here you find luxurious hotels, where the wealthy come to amuse themselves at night, towering only a stone's throw from clusters of slum dwellings made of tattered jute cloth and plastic. Some try, with little success, to address these inequalities, and others accept them as part of life. In this India, where nothing is lost, where both past and present thrive and the future patiently awaits its chance, I was born.

Holding firmly to its traditional values, the village of my birth represents the true spirit of ancient India. The name of this village is Amar Garh. A simple description will help you understand where I come from and the tradition and the culture I embody. The tale of this village will take you back in time, enabling you to understand why, in this land, such a variety of traditions have evolved and how they co-exist even to this day.

Amar Garh is located in one of the most backward areas of Uttar Pradesh, a state in northern India. It is at the hub of a cluster of smaller villages. Even now hundreds of villages in the region lack even the smallest shop where daily necessities, such as oil and soap, can be purchased. But long ago, the village of Amar Garh put aside a piece of land where a bazaar could be held twice a week. Local traders brought their merchandise: grains, vegetables, fabric, lamp oil, spices, yogurt, and cattle. The postman came with his portable post office, and the villagers came from a ten- to fifteen-mile radius to pick up their mail and post letters. When someone was lucky enough to receive a money order, the news spread like wildfire throughout the region. Here in the bazaar, the progressive merchants strengthened their bonds with preferred customers by offering them local raw sugar and a glass of water.

Around the open space where the bazaar was held, houses had been built along passages so narrow that they could hardly be called streets. This congested settlement mirrored the long history of India—from the Stone Age all the way to the age of motorized vehicles—and was home to people from all castes, creeds, and professions. They had the bazaar in common, but otherwise these groups did not mix. Each stayed within their own private world, maintaining their distinct lifestyle and following their unique customs. Although their families may have been living in Amar Garh for hundreds of years, they proudly traced their ancestry to nearby villages.

In this rural metropolis the various tradesmen lived in close proximity to each other without actually mixing— there were distinct areas for carpenters, blacksmiths, goldsmiths, jewelers, weavers, potters, cobblers, tailors, washermen, barbers, drummers, those who pressed oil, those who made sweets, and those who roasted grains.

A typical scene of a village bazaar

A woman making cow dung cake, to be used as fuel

There was also a community of wealthy merchants who owned fabric shops and small grocery stores.

Here, as in the rest of the region, profession was governed by caste. Weavers, cobblers, washermen, and drummers, for example, came from the lowest stratum of society. They were the untouchables. Some of them were even outcaste—neither Hindu nor Muslim but somewhere in between. Carpenters, blacksmiths, goldsmiths, jewelers, potters, barbers, those who made sweets, and those who roasted grains were of a slightly higher caste than the untouchables, but still much lower than merchants and those from the warrior caste. People from the higher castes, such as brahmins, did not live within the precincts of Amar Garh, both because their skills and talents were not for sale and because co-mingling of the castes and associated trades was believed to have a contaminating effect.

The palace of the raja of Amar Garh was outside the settlement. It had all the luxuries: beautiful gardens, a man-made pond and lake, stables for horses and elephants, and halls for music and dancing. Those who served the royal family lived nearby, and the luxurious, pleasure-filled life in and around the palace stood in stark contrast to the austere life of toil and strife in the village. The people of Amar Garh, like the millions of inhabitants of the thousands of villages in this region, shared a common fate: poverty, illiteracy, and oppression from their rajas.

I was born in 1953, a time when India was undergoing a dramatic change—politically, socially, and economically. These changes had a tremendous effect on my family. For generations, my family had been the *raj purohit*—the royal teachers of the state of Amar Garh. In 1947, India gained its independence from Britain, leaving more than fifty thousand rajas to reconcile themselves with this change and to find their place in the newly emerging democracy.

Some were wise enough to foresee what these changes would mean. Others were not. Those who understood the magnitude of the coming changes consulted lawyers and accountants, skillfully planning strategies to secure as much of their wealth as possible. They sold some of their land, transformed at least a section or two of their palaces into hotels, formed companies to juggle their farmlands, and established charitable organizations with themselves as trustees. Some became politicians in the newly democratic nation. After they had consolidated their positions, they voluntarily surrendered their remaining assets to the Indian government. But those who were not so wise reasoned that if the British, on whose empire the sun had never set, could not destroy their sovereignty, then how could this fledgling government, without even a king at its head, take away their kingdoms?

As soon as the British left and India became a democracy, the centuries-old feudal system collapsed. The rajas who had made no attempt to adapt to the changes brought about by democracy were hit hard. The raja of Amar Garh was one of these. He died soon after independence and his ministers, advisers, and managers abandoned the widowed queen. With the help of her personal secretary, the queen struggled to manage her farmlands, which had been reduced to almost nothing, and to maintain the palace on an ever-shrinking income. Within months, all the elephants and horses had been sold, and the queen was left with a handful of attendants in a palace that once housed thousands. The palace could no longer support its cadre of pandits, brahmins, and priests, including my father, its raj purohit.

Growing up in this environment, surrounded by upheaval, I listened to the stories of a golden past, trying to reconcile these tales with the confusion and misery I was seeing around me. People who had once been close to the royal family often sat idle and reminisced about past glories and praised the splendid deeds of their ancestors. Those who had merely been subjects were equally idle, but they passed their time blaming their misfortunes on the royalty and other members of the upper class. Both groups clung to their traditional customs and religious practices, making no real effort to adjust to the new circumstances in which they found themselves.

While I was still quite young, I began questioning the time-honored values of Indian society, which I found great and glorious as well as trivial and meaningless. Looking back on it, it is a mystery how my parents managed to gently push me forward through a society simultaneously stagnant and undergoing dramatic changes.

The palace of Amar Garh

My Parents

Most people living in villages in this part of India were engulfed in utter poverty. In comparison, the members of our extended family were fairly wealthy. The king of Amar Garh had given my forefathers a large tract of farmland. Custom forbade high-class brahmins from working in the fields—this was the job of the lower castes. They plowed our land, looked after our cattle, and took care of all the domestic chores except the kitchen work. In exchange, they received a share of the harvest. My father's daily routine included several hours of meditation in the morning, after which he would make a round of the farmland; in the afternoon, he joined the formal assembly at the palace. As was customary, the members of the royal family gave our family frequent love offerings. These gifts included money, jewelry, clothing, cows, and land. The royal family also took pride in taking care of the wedding expenses of our family members, and they did it lavishly.

In the early 1950s, an act demolishing the rights of landlords was passed. According to this law, the ownership of farmland passed to the one who had been actively working it for seven years or more. This law did not affect the ownership of residences, or the land immediately surrounding them used for domestic purposes, or the orchards. Overnight, the economic status of my family plummeted. The king and the love offering to his royal teacher had already vanished; now the farmland donated to our family long ago was no longer ours. All that remained was our house, garden, cattle, and my mother's jewelry.

Fortunately, in a village about six miles from our house, there was another piece of land being farmed under the supervision of my father's uncle. This remained in the family. After a few years, my father sold it and bought some land near our house, but it was not big enough to provide work for the plowmen and their families who for generations had depended on us for their living. Although our sources of income had diminished drastically, our expenses had not: the plowmen, washermen, the barber, and blacksmith, for example, still came to collect their biannual share of the harvest. And my mother felt obligated to feed the priests and other brahmins and give them love offerings on the numerous holy days that fill the Hindu calendar.

My father had two brothers who were much younger. Despite all the efforts of my grandfather and father, they had gone to school only briefly and had learned to write only well enough to sign their names. They were not yet married and found nothing better to do with their time than busy themselves gossiping with the idle among the villagers. Talking with such people convinced them that my father was raising his five children by using their two-thirds share of the family's wealth. When they expressed their feelings to my father and demanded their share so they could live independently, he was devastated. As the eldest brother, he was head of the extended family. To him, dissatisfaction in the hearts of his brothers was clear evidence that he had failed to fulfill his duty.

Now the house, which was already somewhat run-down, was further defaced by being split into three parts. The farmland and orchards were also divided. I vaguely remember the fight that took place when it came time to divide the four oxen. It was a messy dispute. A host of people from the village came to our home, set themselves up as judges, and offered endless solutions on how to divide the oxen. If it hadn't been so sad, it would have been comical.

Today, having received an education in Western psychology, I understand what was happening to my father.

Pandit Rajpati Tigunait (author's father)

Srimati SubhadraTigunait (author's mother)

Just a few years earlier he had been the most respected person in the village and had been regarded as the wisest man in the entire region. He had long supported religious and charitable projects in the area. On most days he went to the king's court riding his own beautiful horse, but on special occasions, the royal elephant was sent for him. His advice at court was regarded as conclusive. Yet now, during this conflict over a few oxen, he sat speechless, eyes downcast. After this, my father became withdrawn and spent most of his time meditating and reciting scriptures in praise of the Divine Mother.

The rigid caste system dictated that he must maintain his "purity." As a brahmin, all he could do was provide religious counseling and teach, receiving love offerings in return, but that did not provide for his growing family. The only way to meet our daily needs was to sell my mother's jewelry. Thank God there was quite a bit of it. My father felt that selling the jewelry to buy food was disgraceful, so in the beginning he used it to secure a loan. Naturally these were high-interest loans, and as our family had no source of income, my father was never able to repay them. Each time he borrowed money using jewelry as collateral, my father hoped for a miracle that would enable him to redeem it. The interest compounded and the debt doubled, then tripled, until eventually, the jewelry had to be sold. This was done secretly.

None of this stopped my parents from living their lives in the age-old fashion. My father had little involvement in raising the children. As he grew older, he dedicated more and more of his time to spiritual pursuits—more recitation of the scriptures, longer meditations, and more discussions on spiritual matters with those who visited him. My mother cared for my sisters and me, making sure we had breakfast on time, went to school, and worked hard at our studies.

My mother was more orthodox than my father in following the time-honored customs of traditional Hindu society. She had not been to school and could not read or write, but she knew more about gods and goddesses, their temperaments, and how to appease them than my father or any other pandit. She was a person of unmatched discipline. She would never take even a sip of water before she had bathed and performed her daily rituals. With five young children and a husband to take care of, this meant she never had her first bite of food before two in the afternoon. Her spiritual discipline and religious practices consisted of frequent fasting and worshipping different manifestations of God. For example, after taking her bath, she would worship Shiva in the pipal tree, Vishnu in the tulsi plant, and the Divine Mother in the neem tree. Then she offered food to the cows and fed brahmins—normally the members of the families who had traditionally been our priests—before taking her own meal.

My mother was a treasure-house of folklore and the indigenous system of medicine. Her retentive power was mind-boggling. She would tell stories for hours, mostly in lyrics, encouraging us to sing along with her, laughing and giggling, and then ending the stories with simple yet profound lessons.

Fifty years have gone by, but the stories she sang in the local dialect while holding me in her arms still shine in my memory. It was these stories that awakened my desire to discover what was in the vast collection of scriptures that my father had inherited. And it was these same stories that inspired me to learn from my father and the rest of the teachers who later walked into my life.

Pandit Tigunait's mother in her meditation room

The Maze of Time

Life in my village has not changed in a thousand years. Like many villages in northern India it is still untouched by even the basic trappings of the modern world. There are no roads and no electricity, certainly no telephones, televisions, and computers. In the scorching heat of summer, the villagers spend their time threshing wheat, working in the sugarcane fields, and repairing their mud houses. They still pass summer evenings sitting under the trees, discussing ways of curing the symptoms of heatstroke, which they attribute to evil spirits. An outbreak of chicken pox is associated with the wrath of a temperamental goddess, Shitala. The early hours of the night are filled with *pachara*, melodious folk songs dedicated to this goddess, sung by traditional healers. On a specific day during the rainy season, the villagers search for cobras and attempt to strengthen their bonds with these snakes by offering them milk. In the winter, they celebrate the wedding of Lord Vishnu and his consort, sugarcane. The women polish their jewelry and bring it to the fields to adorn the sugarcane and perform the wedding rituals that join Lord Vishnu with the sugarcane. Only when this has been done does the harvest begin.

Social norms and the economic structure in these villages are much the same as they have been for thousands of years. Although the landlords are gone and people from all castes now have the privilege of owning land, the ancient *jajmani* system is still firmly in place. Under this system, everyone in the village is, in one way or another, a client of someone else. Barbers, washermen, blacksmiths, weavers, goldsmiths, carpenters, potters, plowmen, and priests, for example, all exchange services. For all practical purposes, they are dependent on each other, and yet they cling to their age-old rigid caste system. It is unthinkable, for example, for a cobbler to sit on a chair in the house of a brahmin or for a brahmin to drink from the well of a washerman.

The world of the villagers rarely extends more than twenty or thirty miles from their birthplace. Within this world, they are born, grow up, and strengthen their family ties by marrying into the same clans that their forefathers married into. When I was a child, the whole region was drowning in illiteracy. Those who could read and write a simple letter were considered heroes.

In that circumscribed world, there was a woman who taught preschool children in a thatched hut just outside her home. She belonged to an outcaste community known as *nat*, which means "acrobat." The members of this community were not integrated into either Hindu or Muslim society and they were poorer than anyone else in the village. Yet somehow this lady had managed to educate herself. The nomadic ways of her family, who earned their livelihood with acrobatic performances, had enabled her to interact with people beyond the narrow confines of our village, and she had taught herself how to read and write. She was determined to pass these skills on to as many children as possible, but very few families in the village sent their children to her because they feared the association would contaminate their caste purity.

My family had no such concerns. My parents believed that anyone capable of giving knowledge to others is automatically a brahmin. In their view, it is the knowledge and compliance with one's own conscience that qualifies a person as a brahmin. Thus, they sent me to her school, and this great lady, although discarded by the village elite, came to be my first teacher. I was so young that I don't remember exactly what I learned there, but I have a faint memory of playing and singing with her and the other children. Today, as I tax my memory, I see myself as a child smeared with dust, running around my teacher's goat as she tried to teach me a poem composed by Mahatma Gandhi:

> *My Lord Rama, Thou art the Master of all living beings.*
> *Thou art the one who uplifts the downtrodden.*
> *Ishvara and Allah are Thy names.*
> *O Almighty Inner Light, please bless all*
> *   with right understanding.*

The "Untouchable" Healer

In my village, there lived an elderly man named Chinigi. By caste, he was *chamar*—an untouchable. He did not own a single inch of farmland; he earned his livelihood as a plowman. He worked hard and lived a simple life. In addition to being a skilled plowman, he was an expert in building mud houses, raising cattle, and digging wells. Most of all, he was a famed healer. I have yet to see a person as disciplined in maintaining a daily routine. In all seasons, he woke up at the same time and walked a mile for his morning ablution—he brushed his teeth and cleaned his throat and nostrils. Then he did some stretching, bathed with cold water, recited his prayers, and went to attend the oxen and the plow of his master—everything perfectly on time. People of higher castes mocked his disciplined life. "A *chamar*, untouchable by birth, living a pious and flawless life?" they taunted. "So successful in reversing the law of God!"

Even as an old man, Chinigi faithfully observed a vow that he had taken during early adulthood. When he was a young man, he lit a ceremonial fire and kept it burning continuously ever since. At the end of each day, when he returned from his work, he would walk a mile or more for his evening ablution, and then return home and gather sticks and dry cow dung to feed his ceremonial fire. Then he sat down beside the fire, and people lay their problems before him. His visitors—of all castes, creeds, ages, and genders—would come seeking a cure for coughs, colds, fevers, diarrhea, rashes, and eye and ear infections, all of which they attributed to ghosts, spirits, and the evil eye. He would pick up a pinch of warm ash from his fireplace, put it on his left palm, and while rubbing it with his right thumb, would mentally repeat a healing mantra. As soon as he began repeating the mantra, he became a different person. His countenance changed, and depending on how sick the patient was, his eyes watered and he would yawn. With each repetition, he would take a touch of the ash from his palm with his thumb and forefinger and blow it toward the patient. He always did this seven times. Three visits were more than enough for a lasting cure, and yet this healer was treated as an untouchable.

It bothered me that even those who came seeking his blessings treated him as an outcaste. I wondered how it was possible to receive healing grace from someone whom you keep so far away from your heart. When I asked my father this question, he said, "The healing grace flows through him because he loves all and hates none. His heart is open to God and to all of creation. His love is so pure and so perfect that he has power to open others' hearts regardless of whether they notice their hearts opening or not. There is no flaw in him. He is a perfect conduit for divine love."

Today, having traveled far and wide, meeting hundreds of learned and holy men from a myriad of traditions and faiths, I realize that this simple villager was a great man. Yet people were so entangled in their web of customs, dogmas, and prejudices that they could not see what was right before their eyes. This man could have given them infinitely more than a pinch of ash to relieve their maladies, but all they could see in him was a lowly untouchable.

My First School

When I was seven, my father took me to the primary school a mile and a half from our home. It was funded by the government and ran from first grade to fifth. The school consisted of a one-room building that served both as a classroom and as an administrative office. This building was surrounded by a big courtyard. Outside the courtyard were a few trees, under which additional classes were held. There were five hundred children and three teachers.

That first day the headmaster brought out his thick enrollment register. After writing my name and my parents' names, he asked about my birth date. My father remembered my birth date according to the lunar calendar, but the school was operated under the British system of education and required my birth date according to the Christian calendar. Neither my father nor the headmaster knew how to translate one calendar into the other. Finally the headmaster decided my birth date fell somewhere between January and May, and eventually the two agreed I had been born on January 15. That evening I remember arguing with my father about this. Several times in the past I had asked him why some people cannot tolerate the cold of winter. He had always replied that those born in the winter are comfortable with the cold while those born in the summer prefer hot weather. I had never liked the cold, and so, relying on my father's wisdom, I came to believe I had been born in the summer. A birth date of January 15—the peak of winter in India—did not seem right to me. I argued with my father until he ordered me to be quiet. "What difference does it make?" he said. "The name and the birth date written in the school's register does not affect one's providence." To this day, I still don't know the date of my birth.

Pandit Tigunait's first school

The first few months at school were hard—five hundred children and only a few cared anything about learning. I missed my preschool teacher, who had admired me and let me play. Discipline here was based on punishment—there were no rewards. But as soon as I learned to read and write, going to school became a source of pleasure. I was over-joyed at the prospect of reading all of my father's books and proving to him that I knew everything he knew. I also cherished the ambition of reading his books to my mother. As a first-grader I had already memorized the multiplication tables all the way to forty and quickly learned to read the Hindi version of the *Ramayana* and recite dozens of verses written in Sanskrit. This amazed my teachers.

The news that I was a good student spread through the village, and people looked up to me. This had both a positive and a negative effect: the appreciation of the teachers and the people in the village inspired me to study harder, but I was not motivated to play with children my own age. As a result, I felt adults loved me but children regarded me as an odd duck.

My teachers were pleased with my progress. Within six months they promoted me to the second grade. By the time the first academic year ended I was in third grade. The following year, I completed both third and fourth grade, and in my third year at school, I completed fifth grade.

Due to my studious tendencies I did not mix well with most of the other children. The few friends I did make were left behind every six months when I was moved into a new grade. My rapid progress separated me from my friends while inciting envy among some of the other children. This was obvious from their actions. For example, they would steal another child's pencil, hide it in my backpack, and then expose me as the thief. It seemed pointless to go to the teachers because they would look at the evidence, and the evidence would be in favor of those who were in the majority and shouted the loudest. When I told my mother about these goings-on, she simply said I was a good and brave boy, and that she was proud of me. If she noticed I was still downcast, she would send me to my father, who would simply say, "Such things happen in school. Very soon you will be out of that environment."

In the past thirty years, values have changed in India. But when I was growing up, parents stayed out of children's lives in school, leaving that to the teachers. The atmosphere at school was sterile and austere, and discipline simply meant obeying orders lest you be punished or expelled. This atmosphere made most students either rebellious or timid. Somehow I was spared both of these unpleasant fates.

Ghosts

My primary school was a mile from home, and to reach it I had to cross a fifty-acre mango orchard. In the middle of that orchard was a monument where the king of Amar Garh had been cremated. According to local belief, he had turned into a ghost who from time to time ran through the orchard and nearby farms in the form of a gigantic buffalo or a huge bull. Other ghosts often came to join the king, usually traveling in the form of snakes. But in the summertime, the ghosts took the form of dust devils. If a dust devil was big, people assumed it was the *raja saheb,* the king himself. To the villagers, and especially to the children, these stories were so credible that the very idea of snakes, roaming bulls, and dust devils was terrifying. I was no exception.

During the summer, after the crops are harvested and the land is completely dry, all that remains is dust and dry leaves. Dust devils are common and carry so much dust and debris that even the smallest appear formidable. We encountered these dust devils almost every day on our way home from school. Upon seeing them, most of the children ran away. A few believed that the ghosts were repelled by the smell of onions—they carried onions in their pockets and were bold enough to ignore the dust devils and continue on their way. Upon seeing them walking so fearlessly, I went to my mother and asked for an onion. Instead of giving me one, she said, "The ghosts living in the dust devils have no power to harm you. Don't be dependent on onions for your protection. You know the *Hanuman Chalisa* [forty couplets dedicated to the god Hanuman]. Whenever you are afraid, simply recite these prayers. You will become strong, and the dust devils will run away. But if they are so close that you don't have time to recite all forty couplets, imagine that your head is at the feet of Lord Hanuman and simply start repeating the particular verse that protects you from ghosts."

The next time I was confronted by one of these dust devils, I stood firm and recited the *Hanuman Chalisa*. The dust devil did not come near me, so I was convinced that the prayer worked. My mind was not yet contaminated by logic, and so I did not reason that the dust devils were caused by differences in temperature and that was why they traveled from one orchard to another. Instead, I was proud of my mother's wisdom and happy that she shared it with me. My faith in Hanuman and in this set of prayers dedicated to him grew tremendously. My fear of ghosts living in dust devils, and even the ghosts which according to local belief lived in all deserted and dark places, vanished forever.

Like hunger, thirst, and sleep, fear is a natural urge in all living beings. It is instinctual, and manifests in varying grades and degrees when our innate urge of self-preservation is triggered. Under proper guidance, fear can be transformed into faith and inner strength. In fact, this is the purpose of spiritual training.

A More Powerful God

Childhood is the age of faith. Logic and reasoning have very little influence on a child. I loved Hanuman, the mighty god who protected me from ghosts traveling as dust devils and spirits who lived in dark places. My favorite prayer in those days was *Hanuman Chalisa.*

Then one day I heard a story about how Hanuman had dedicated his life in the service of Lord Rama. I also heard and read a score of stories about amazing feats Hanuman had performed in service of his master. He crossed hundreds of miles of ocean in one gigantic leap. In Sri Lanka, he fought and defeated thousands of powerful demons all by himself, burned the entire city, and returned to his master unharmed. When Rama's brother was wounded in the battlefield on the island of Sri Lanka, Hanuman flew all the way to the Himalayas and brought back not just a few medicinal plants but the whole mountain peak where these plants were growing. And he did it in one night.

If Hanuman had so much power then how much power his master Lord Rama must have! In my innocence, I thought that receiving the grace of Rama was a higher achievement than being protected by his devoted servant Hanuman. This led me to study the *Ramayana,* India's most celebrated scripture, and the practices it describes.

I now realize how childish it is to think that one god is higher than another and that receiving the grace of a "higher" god is a higher achievement. But even though this was a mistaken belief, it inspired me to commit myself to the study and practice of the *Ramayana,* which in turn became a lifelong source of knowledge and inspiration.

It doesn't matter how we start our quest; what really matters is that we start, and through sustained study, self-reflection, and methodical practice, we continue refining our understanding of the meaning and purpose of life.

chapter one

The Power of Superstition

My father was very fond of books. He was a Sanskrit
scholar, and he considered preserving scriptures, especially
those in manuscript form, to be his spiritual and moral duty.
His private collection far exceeded the number of ancient
texts found in many of the famous libraries of north India.
My parents later told me that even as a child I was attracted
to those books. As soon as I learned to read, the room where
the books were kept became my favorite place. In primary
school, there was no homework so I had plenty of time to
browse through my father's books. By the time I was in fifth
grade, I had already read a couple hundred scriptures that
had been translated into Hindi and had fallen in love with
one of the most celebrated, the *Mahabharata*.

The *Mahabharata* is a voluminous work, bigger than
Homer's the *Iliad* and the *Odyssey* combined. It is a de-
tailed account of a historic war that took place in India almost 6,000 years ago. While narrating the story of two
opposing kings, the author, the great sage Vyasa, expounds
on history, geography, philosophy, politics, ethics, morality,
psychology, mythology, spirituality, and metaphysics in
a style that is simple, yet elegant. When I had questions
about what I was reading, I sought clarification from my
father, and was amazed to discover that he had inherited
stories from the oral tradition that had been omitted from
this scripture. Years later, it was these stories that helped
me find the proper frame for the practices described in this
and other scriptures.

By the time I was eight or nine, it had become my habit
to take one of the volumes of the *Mahabharata* (the copy in
my father's collection ran many volumes) and read it whenever I got the chance. One day, while I was immersed in the

story, one of my uncles burst into the room. Somehow he had found out that I was reading the *Mahabharata,* and he was furious. When he saw me reading one of the volumes, he shouted, "You have already brought enough fighting and misery to our family by reading this book. I do not want to see this book in your hand ever again!" He snatched the volume I had been reading and hurled it into the corner of the room.

My mother witnessed this incident, but knowing that if she said anything to my uncle, he would become even more violent, she remained quiet. I did not want to bother my father by telling him what my uncle had done, but I did ask him what my uncle meant by saying I had brought fighting and misery to our family by reading this book. My father replied, "The war described in the *Mahabharata* caused so much devastation and misery that for many people even a passing mention of it evokes terror. In the dark age of Indian history that began when this war ended, the belief arose that any reference to that war creates a contentious atmosphere that will lead inevitably to another war. Your uncle, along with millions of other people, is suffering from this baseless superstition."

After this episode, I tried to read this text as unobtrusively as possible. But one day, my uncle caught me red-handed. He slapped and punched me and threw me against the wall. But that was nothing compared to what he did next. He snatched the volume I'd been reading and tore it to shreds. Then he grabbed the other volumes from the shelf, ripped off the covers, and tore them to pieces, yelling at me while I watched, transfixed. By the time my father arrived, the entire scripture had been destroyed.

Many people are spellbound by the power of superstition. They go on believing what they have been taught and doing what they have seen others do, without stopping to examine the validity of such beliefs and actions. Such blind beliefs kill our courage to explore the truth beyond the confines of our narrow world. Thus we go on living stagnant lives, harming ourselves and others.

Providence Has Its Way

When I completed fifth grade, my father had to make a big decision: Should I go to a school for formal education or learn about scriptures from him and become a pandit? Royal patrons of traditional knowledge were gone. The new rulers of democratic India were the politicians, who busied themselves with party politics, much of which centered around exploiting caste and community sentiments. They had little time to promote ancient wisdom and values. If I followed in my father's footsteps and became a pandit, the only way I could earn a living would be to perform rituals for others and earn my livelihood by collecting love offerings. In a society where old values were disintegrating and new ones were not yet formed, the profession of performing rituals was just like begging, only in religious garb.

My father had already come to the conclusion that I must study subjects that would help me adjust to this changing world and that I must get a diploma so I could earn a decent living. I knew how painful it was for him to see his son abandon the family tradition and to disregard his own moral obligation to preserve and pass on what he had inherited from his ancestors. After a few discussions, he decided that I should go to a regular middle school. Now the problem was how to get me admitted to a full-fledged middle school where many of the modern subjects that I wanted to study were taught.

There was a school only two miles away from my home, running from sixth through twelfth grade, that taught all the subjects I wanted to learn. I had good marks in fifth grade and could easily get into this school, but it was too expensive. The monthly fee of five rupees (approximately one dollar) was too much for our family to afford.

Then there was another school four miles away, and that
one ran from sixth through eighth grade. The manager of
this school was a friend of my father's and had promised
him that my fee would be waived. This was a great incen-
tive, and so I was enrolled in that school.

In reality, however, this second establishment could
hardly qualify as a school. In the place of a permanent
building, it had a few thatched huts. The manager always
struggled to pay the teachers' salaries, which were so meager it was almost a joke. However, there was a highly
dedicated teacher, Babu Bhulan Singh, who, through his
effort and influence, managed to keep the other teachers
interested in offering their services, regardless of whether
or not they received their salary. Despite his sincere efforts,
quite often the teachers quit, new ones came, and during
these transitions Babu Bhulan Singh would substitute for
them all. On those occasions, at least two-thirds of the
students enrolled in that school did pretty much whatever
they wished. Students who lacked self-motivation and
self-supervision—and that was the majority—either sat
idly, or mobbed cucumber and sugarcane fields and
orchards of neighboring villagers.

I did not like to involve myself in such activities, but
occasionally I gave in to peer pressure. One memorable
occasion occurred toward the end of my first year of
middle school. Some of us were sitting under a tree gossiping
and snacking on roasted grains. One of our friends lectured
us on the nutritious value of the resin of the acacia tree: "The
resin of the acacia tree is superb for vitality, virility, and
memory. You can never have back pain, and if you eat it
daily, you can compete in high jumping and you will see
that you have springs in your knees." Another fellow, who
always posed as the smartest, added, "Oh yes, Nawab of
Lucknow ate it every day and that is how he managed his

360 wives!" We laughed and measured the strength of our muscles in our arms and thighs, and with no minds at all, we set out to gather the resin of the acacia tree.

There was a monastery a mile from the school. Located on a hundred-acre piece of land, it was surrounded by a lush forest of trees and bushes, mainly tamarind, flame-of-the-forest, and acacia. Skillfully avoiding the thorns on the acacia bushes, we entered the forest, and before we knew it, we were lost. As for acacia resin, we hardly gathered a fistful. We were hungry and thirsty and scared to death that we would never get out of that jungle. We tried to find our way back to the school by sheer guesswork, but instead ended up on the other side of the forest near the monastery. As soon as we heard voices, we ran, terrified of being caught. As we crashed through the brush, dogs joined the chase. I was the smallest in the group, and not wanting to be ripped apart by the dogs, I climbed a flame-of-the-forest tree and sat on a limb while the dogs snarled and barked underneath. One of the sadhus from the monastery came to see why the dogs were barking, and there I was.

The monk called off the dogs and took me to the monastery. There I saw the head of the monastery, Baba Fular Das, sitting in the courtyard. He was a childhood friend of my father, and even after becoming a monk, frequently visited our home, so we recognized each other instantly. When he asked me what I was doing in the tree, I told him the whole story. Baba Fular Das laughed and said, "I have asked your father so many times to let you stay here at the monastery and not waste time walking eight miles a day, but he doesn't listen to me." The sadhu who had spotted me hiding in the tree said, "It's because his father thinks that it is not appropriate for a householder to use the resources of a monastery . . ." Cutting him off

The monastery outside Amar Garh

mid-sentence, the head monk said with a laugh, "No, no, his father fears that if his young son lives here, he might develop a taste for monastic life."

Baba Fular Das gave me some sweets and water, and when I had regained my composure, he took me to the center of the property and showed me the man-made pond which local people called *sagar,* "the ocean." The monastery had been built by the king of Amar Garh as a temporary residence for his spiritual master, Bengali Baba, the grand-master of this present monk. Bengali Baba, who was also known as Baba Dharam Das, was very fond of mountains and forests, so the king had created an artificial mountain by building a high dirt berm around the pond and foresting it with a variety of trees. He had also set concrete structures into the berm to create a cave-like atmosphere. The head monk lovingly showed me every nook and cranny of this place, but it was those caves that impressed me the most.

When I returned home that evening, I told my father what had happened. Upon hearing my story, he recited a verse from the *Ramayana,* "O Lord, you may assign me to the lowest rung of hell for as long as you wish, but please prevent me from being in bad company." Even this much, coming from my father's mouth, was enough to shake my being and set me straight. The next day, the head monk visited my father. I do not remember what else they talked about, but I do remember my father saying, "Fular Dasji, destiny has its own way. Despite the fact that he ran amok, was chased by dogs, and hid in a tree, he was rescued by a saint and was led to a monastery. There must be some reason in it."

From that time on, I was so drawn to the monastery that I found excuses to go there whenever I could. This became easier when I was in eighth grade, when Baba Fular Das gave my teacher a room, a small kitchen, and other facilities at the monastery for his use. Then Baba Fular Das attempted to convince my father that it was important that I stay at the monastery so that I could study with this excellent teacher and prepare properly for my final exams. At that time, the school I was attending had not been certified by the education board, but we could sit for the exams as private students. The more students from the school who passed with high grades, the better the school's chances for becoming certified, so the teacher encouraged me to ask my father to allow me to study at night with him at the monastery. Finally, my father gave his permission and during my last few months in middle school I began to spend most of my nights at the monastery. During this time Baba Fular Das told me countless stories about saints and yogis. He even taught me a few breathing exercises.

My desire to learn breathing exercises had been kindled by what I thought was a miraculous occurrence. Twelve years earlier, Baba Fular Das had ordained a monk, who—following the rules of the tradition—then left the monastery to wander freely for twelve years. During that time, he was to do a certain practice, and when the practice was completed, he was to return to the monastery, bringing with him a contribution to the annual feast. A month before the feast day, the monk arrived in our village, displaying a unique talent. As he walked through the village he played two flutes, one with each nostril. This drew everyone's attention. He walked to a nearby pond, followed by a large crowd. There, to everyone's astonishment, he walked out on the water and seated himself in lotus pose, all the while playing the two flutes. Then he got up and walked on the water back to shore. Everyone prostrated at his feet. He told the villagers he needed some grain and money for the annual feast at the monastery. The crowd not only contributed what he asked, but carried the load to the monastery for him.

I was present during the feast. This particular sadhu and his flutes were the central attraction—people treated him like a celebrity. I was fascinated. The day after the feast, this sadhu left the monastery to continue his wandering. One evening I asked Baba Fular Das how this sadhu could walk on water—and sit on it—without sinking. The head monk explained that he had mastered a special practice called *plavini mudra* and had meditated on a special mantra. As a result, he could levitate. When I asked him whether I could learn this practice, he replied that I was too young and that my top priority was to attend to my studies. But he did tell me a number of startling stories associated with his grandmaster, Baba Dharam Das. Those stories were fantastic. But whenever I asked him to teach me some of the practices he had learned from his master and grandmaster, he would simply say, "Complete your studies, learn the scriptures, and gain knowledge so that you can distinguish real spiritual experience from mere magic and tricks."

Wine Turns to Milk

The run-down palace of the king of Amar Garh stood just a quarter of a mile away from the trail leading to my school. One morning, several of us were walking along the path on our way to school when we heard a deep thundering sound. Then we saw a cloud of dust rising from the ground with hundreds of pigeons emerging from it. Curious, we ran toward the cloud and discovered that the western portion of the three-story palace had collapsed. We stood there, awed and bewildered. The people who lived nearby kept their distance, fearing the remaining portion of the palace would collapse at any moment. One remarked, "I hope the eastern portion doesn't collapse; otherwise, the poor queen . . ." Another fellow gave a long sigh and said, "It had to happen. Sooner or later your karma gets you." I didn't understand these remarks.

That evening, I told my father what I had seen and heard that morning and asked if he knew what the people gathered there were talking about. "Yes," he replied, and told me the following story:

The king of Amar Garh was fond of the number twenty-four. He had twenty-four wrestlers, twenty-four pandits, twenty-four dancers, twenty-four horses, and so on. One of the twenty-four pandits was a tantric who worshipped the goddess Kali with ritual ingredients that included wine and meat. He performed his ritual worship in the palace temple.

One day, a sadhu from the Kabira order visited the palace. In the tradition of Saint Kabira, the usage of wine is strictly prohibited. The eldest prince and his admirers fell under the influence of this sadhu, and during the several weeks that he stayed at the palace, the members of the royal family gradually became divided into two groups: one admired this sadhu, and the other continued supporting the tantric pandit who used wine in his ritual worship. Since the power was in the hands of the eldest prince, the majority became antagonistic toward any form of religious or esoteric practice involving wine, and the tantric pandit became the target of increasing animosity. The group around the eldest prince watched this adept constantly and criticized him mercilessly. "He is creating an impure environment in the palace," they would say. "How can anyone justify indulgence and orgies as a spiritual practice? It is nonsense. We should inform the king." Eventually they made a formal complaint to the king.

Although the king had known all along about the pandit's ritual practices, he called him before an assembly and asked if he drank wine. The pandit replied, "I do not indulge in liquor; rather, I worship the Divine Mother in a manner prescribed in the scripture." When someone asked why he locked the door when he performed the worship, he answered, "This kind of practice is done in private. This is not a ritual worship that priests perform and devotees observe. It is open only to the initiates." The king was satisfied with the explanation and adjourned the assembly.

But the prince's sycophants did not give up. Intent on exposing this pandit and his use of alcohol in worshipping the Goddess, they followed him and found out where he got the wine and when the secret worship began. One night, when the pandit had begun his worship, the prince and his followers surrounded the temple, and pounding at the door, demanded admittance. The pandit was in the middle of the ritual, and there was a strict rule against exposing this particular practice to anyone. When the racket continued, not knowing what else to do, he prayed to the Goddess to forgive him for concluding the practice inappropriately. Then he said, "Mother, I am your child. Do as you wish." With this prayer, he opened the door. The group rushed in but found only milk in the chalices. The whole group stormed out in frustration. This great mystic, who had seen the wine turning into milk before his eyes, exclaimed in gratitude, "Oh Mother, you went out of your way to protect me. What good is this place where you have to go through such trouble?" The next morning, he resigned from the king's service, and many other pandits followed him.

"Before long," my father told me, "a series of calamities began: Fatal accidents befell the royal family, and diseases and disputes arose among them. In a matter of a few months, landlordship was abolished, and the royal family lost its property. Sections of the palace collapsed one at a time. The portion of the palace that collapsed today was infested by rats and snakes, and overrun with pigeons."

I asked my father if the tantric had put a curse on the royal family and if he himself had the power to curse someone. Normally, my father ignored such questions, but this time he replied briefly, "Such adepts are blessed children of the Divine Mother. If someone hurts you in front of me or your mother, will we be able to tolerate it?"

Then I asked, "Who is this Divine Mother? How can I seek and find her protection?"

"She is the Mother of all," he replied. "She is in you, in me, and in everyone. She is everywhere. She is the true source of protection and nourishment. In all situations and circumstances, she guides and protects us. Once you come to know that you are always under her loving care, you will not have any fear."

Since that day, I have longed to know more about the Divine Mother, who, in the words of my father, is the source of true protection and nurturance.

CHAPTER TWO
I Find My Way

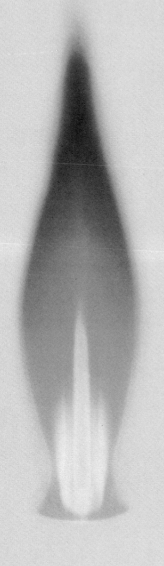

The Forbidden Scripture

I took my final exams and felt a great sense of relief, but not for long. It took a minimum of forty days to get the results, and although I was confident my marks would be high, the horror stories that go along with junior high and high school final exams made sleep difficult. For their final exams, students are sent to other schools, where the security is intense. If you are caught cheating, you are doomed. If you fail, your destiny is decided: you collect cow dung and are thankful to God for a piece of bread at the end of the day. If you pass with low grades, you will be admitted to high school, but in the Art Side—stuck with subjects like history, Sanskrit, geography, civics, and home science. If you graduate in these subjects, you may get a job carrying tea cups from office to office, and if fate really favors you, you may become a clerk and can live with some measure of dignity. But if you pass your eighth-grade exams with honors, then you have the chance to go in the Science Side, where you can take math, physics, chemistry, botany, and zoology, and start dreaming about the day you will become an engineer, a doctor, a scientist, a high-ranking government official, or CEO of a company, make lots of money, and enjoy the goddess of prosperity kissing your feet. You can imagine what I was hoping for.

During the long summer vacation that followed the exams, I had plenty of time to browse through my father's large collection of books and recite prayers to win the favor of Lord Hanuman—not to overcome the fear of ghosts this time, but for high grades on my exams. I also recited prayers to Lord Rama with the child-like logic that I should do something in case granting high honors was beyond the capacity of Hanuman. And I did something else as well. From childhood, I had been observing the special love and devotion my father had for the Divine Mother. He never let anyone near him when he did his ritual worship and meditation on the goddess Durga, except at the end of the practice when he called us to take *prasad* (blessed fruits or sweets). I had always wanted to know what he did so privately—I knew it must be very esoteric. I imagined that his practice and the particular scripture he recited as part of his daily worship were more precious than anything in the world. My father's friend, Baba Fular Das, had often told me that I did not need to go far in search of divine help—the monastery was nearby, he himself was there, and my father was right there in our home. Just a few months earlier, after my father had told me the story of the Goddess turning wine into milk, he had said emphatically, "Once you come to know that you are always under her loving care, you will not have any fear." These words and the desire to have a bright and secure future gave me courage to read the sacred scripture that my father held in such high esteem, even though I had the sense that it might be forbidden to everyone except him.

One day, when no one was around, I sneaked into my father's meditation room. In the dim light of the lamp, I saw his scripture wrapped in red cloth with a few hibiscus flowers lying on top. I closed the door, unwrapped the scripture, and began reading. It was fascinating. There were clusters of mantras for general protection, purification, and propitiation of nature's forces. Then there were preparatory practices that were prerequisites for reading the scripture. The scripture itself consisted of thirteen chapters, and these chapters were further divided into three parts. Each part was dedicated to propitiating different aspects of the Divine Mother—Kali, Lakshmi, and Sarasvati. I read the whole book in a couple of hours. Then I wrapped it in the cloth and put it back.

The rest of the day and into the night, I pondered what I had read:

"It is through her grace one attains success here and spiritual freedom hereafter." I also remembered the promise I had read there: "Through her grace, a student gains knowledge; the poor, wealth; a woman, beauty; and a weak person becomes strong like a bull. Through her grace, a sinking ship begins to float. A defeated king recaptures his kingdom. And a man, once discarded by all, is hailed in the highest glory. Devotees with childish minds seek her grace and beg for petty boons, which she grants generously. But the wise ones pray for her mercy, and upon receiving it, offer it back at her lotus feet. In return, they receive the highest good—everlasting joy and divine protection."

The next day, I opened the scripture again. This time, I read less and contemplated more. From time to time, I made a few notes although with deep discomfort that this might be trivializing the scripture. This secret reading continued for almost a week.

Then one evening, my father asked me quietly, "Do you wash your hands and feet when you read this scripture?"

Surprised, I said, "You knew what I was doing but you didn't say anything?"

He replied, "Why should I say? Scriptures are for those who read them."

"What about the practices?" I asked.

He replied, "They are for those who practice them."

Then I asked, "Will you teach me?"

"Why not?"

He taught me the 108 names of the Divine Mother, and then he said, "The practice based on this scripture requires that you know the Sanskrit language well and are sure that your pronunciation is correct. Once you gain more knowledge of Sanskrit and study the grammar, you will be able to undertake this practice safely and successfully. Study of a scripture is totally different from the recitation, which constitutes an integral part of the spiritual practice. You may continue studying this text so that you can expand your knowledge, but do not recite it without preparatory practices, proper rituals, and most important, without a formal initiation from a competent master."

The more I read this scripture, the more I lost my desire to become a scientist, a CEO, and a rich man, and the less I cared about whether I would spend my days collecting cow dung or enter a profession. All I wanted to know was how it would feel to receive her grace, and how it would feel to live without fear and worry. For that, I knew I had to go to a Sanskrit school, so I no longer cared if I secured the highest honor or the lowest grade in my middle school exams. Today, as I look back, I realize that this dramatic shift in my attitude was a result of divine grace. It came to me even before I began walking toward it.

The Language of Gods

It was 1967. Just three years earlier I had not wanted to go to a traditional Sanskrit school, but now that was all I wanted. Even though I had not yet received my eighth-grade exam results, I made a casual visit to the Sanskrit school just three miles from our home. I wanted to see how it looked, and if possible, to meet the principal, a man my father held in high regard.

It was the beginning of the monsoon season. Just before I reached the school, I had to cross a stream that the heavy rain had turned into a wide river. In those days, not knowing the price of life, I was more courageous than I am today. Using a narrow, flimsy, temporary bridge made of bamboo, I crossed the raging water, avoiding a couple of water snakes who, in an attempt to defeat death, were clinging to this makeshift bridge.

The school, which rested on a high dirt berm bordering a man-made pond, was surrounded on three sides by flood-water. It consisted of a two-room brick building and a mud house with a roof of sugarcane leaves. In the center of the campus stood a gigantic pipal tree that was home to flocks of parrots, sparrows, crows, and nightingales. On the periphery of the campus were all kinds of trees, plants, shrubs, and vines, some wild and some cultivated. In contrast to the floodwater that engulfed the whole region, this little landmass looked like Noah's Ark—a perfect and secure shelter. There under the pipal tree, the principal was sitting on a wooden cot with ten or twelve of his students seated on the ground around him. I took off my rain shoes some distance away, walked humbly through the circle of students, and reverently placed my head at the feet of the teacher. When he put his hand on my head and asked who

The traditional Sanskrit school known as Sanskrit Pathashala

I was, I introduced myself. When I mentioned my father's name, he put his hand a second time on my head and said, "Bless you, bless you, bless you. You are three years late, but finally you are here. How is your father? How is the family? And tell me, what brought you here?"

"I want to study Sanskrit," I replied.

He laughed and said, "Weren't your father's books enough? Have you read them all? What if there is nothing new here?"

Then he told the other students, "Since he started crawling, he has been reading books. His father is a great friend of mine."

The principal asked me to sit down and opened his big astrology book. After a few minutes of silence, he asked one of his students to get the other pandit who was teaching in the brick building. I later came to know that this teacher was one of the greatest astrologers of his time. He was also an expert in palmistry, the science of breath, and a unique branch of astrology and tantra known as *duti vijnana*. The principal asked him whether this was an auspicious moment in which to start my education. He stood a few moments, deeply absorbed in thought, and said, "Right now is the best time to undertake any auspicious endeavor."

At this, the principal taught me the first verse that every Sanskrit student memorizes as part of his or her first lesson. Since my father sang this verse as part of our evening prayers, I already knew it. Then the principal gave me the next lesson and then the next. This went on for almost two hours. From time to time he would say, "Do you know that this is one month of lessons? Two months of lessons?" This inspired me. I thought that within a matter of a few weeks or months, I would catch up with what I had missed in the past three years. Finally, the principal dismissed the other students. I stayed with both teachers for a few minutes, and then I touched their feet in farewell and walked to the gate. There I saw that the floodwater had risen by two feet, and the bamboo bridge was underwater. The two teachers, who were watching from the roof, called me back and invited me to stay with them until the flood receded. Three nights passed before I could cross the river and go home.

I had not told my parents I was visiting the school, so when I did not come home at the end of the first day, people began searching for me throughout the village. The next day, the search widened to encompass the nearby monastery and all my family's relatives and friends. When I returned on the fourth day, I told my parents about my adventures and studies with the two pandits. As usual, my father listened patiently, and at the end of my story, said simply, "May the Mother's will prevail."

Shortly after that, I received the results of my eighth-grade exams—I had passed with high honors. On this basis, I could have been admitted to ninth grade in the Sanskrit school, but my teacher advised me to start from the beginning so that my foundation would be solid and so I would have the full experience of learning Sanskrit in the authentic and traditional way. Thank God I had already absorbed considerable knowledge of Sanskrit from my family background. So I was able to complete the entire course of study from the beginning up to eighth grade in a year. Then I was officially entitled to take an exam that would allow me to enroll in the formal course of Sanskrit study that was regulated and recognized by the Sanskrit University of Banaras. This, too, I passed with honors.

The Sanskrit school became my second home. The principal, whom we lovingly called Bade Guruji (the head *gurudeva*), was a living example of the ancient sages—an embodiment of selfless love, self-sacrifice, and kindness.

The school had only recently been recognized by the education board as an approved educational institution, which meant the teachers received a salary from the government. Prior to this, the principal had been teaching the students free of charge. Even though there were now several teachers, all of them his old students, he still ran the school in the time-honored fashion. He treated the salary as a love offering and shared it with all those who were in need. The classroom was his living room; a corner of the classroom was his meditation room; and when he cooked his main meal the students gathered the firewood, did the prepping, and cleaned his dishes. He made sure that every student, as well as the teachers, had their meal. Just as in the olden days, he performed ritual ceremonies for others, and his students took part in them on his behalf.

Bade Guruji's private life was extremely simple and disciplined. He dedicated several hours in the early morning to meditation, and, like my father, his meditation consisted of ritual worship of the Divine Mother, recitation of the scripture, and *japa* (mantra repetition). He allowed only the most disciplined students to assist him in preparing for the rituals—gathering flowers, making sandalwood paste, arranging sticks in the sacred fireplace, and cleaning ritual utensils. One day when he was not feeling well, he bestowed the highest blessings on me: he told me to perform the ritual worship of the Goddess on the altar where he had been worshipping her for the last sixty years, and to recite the scripture on his behalf (he was now eighty years old). Many of his students, especially those who had now become teachers, were astonished. Being young, I did not realize that this was the greatest privilege he had ever given to a student. When I shared this experience with my father, he acknowledged my good fortune by saying, "I am grateful to him. In his own, mysterious way, today he initiated you into the practice of Shakti worship. From now on, continue doing it just as you did there."

My Sanskrit teacher resides in the deepest recess of my heart. The love I received from him is like an eternal flame that continues to illuminate and nurture the student within me. Whenever I remember this great soul, my heart begins to pulsate with a prayer, "May I ever remain a student so that I may continue tasting the sweetness of his love until eternity."

The Goddess in the Compost Pit

I was in the third year of my Sanskrit schooling, and the Sanskrit school was the center of my universe. I was spending eight to ten hours a day, seven days a week, at the school. I hardly knew what was going on in my village or even at home, although I did know that my father had lost all aptitude for domestic affairs. It was my mother who made sure that the children were well fed, the cattle were attended to, the farmland plowed, and the crops harvested on time. My father attended his scriptures and his Divine Mother, and had an occasional discussion on spiritual matters with those who visited him.

Like anywhere in the world, there were a few people in my village who bullied others. Our village bullies—five brothers—were my distant uncles. Only one of them had gone to school and none were married. All were proud of their big muscles, and in the village, where the majority of the people lived hand to mouth, they displayed their power by keeping the villagers from watering their farmlands so that they could water theirs first. Sometimes they even usurped others' crops.

These men owned a piece of land behind our house. Every year, they encroached on our property by a couple of feet. My parents reminded them repeatedly that they were occupying land that was not theirs, but they didn't listen. By the time I was sixteen, they had devoured so much of our land that they were approaching the outer wall of our house. On that side of the house there were some banana plants and a neem tree. To further enlarge their field, the brothers would need to cut down the trees—and that's what they did.

Chopping down the banana plants was easy and took only a few minutes. But cutting a neem tree is more difficult, and as soon as they started chopping, dozens of people noticed. My father was not around, so the report went to my mother, who came out of the house and protested. One of the brothers shouted at her, "Get out of here, woman, or I will chop you into pieces, too!" It was early morning, and I was getting ready to take a bath. Not knowing what was going on, I came out of my house with an empty bucket, and when I saw the small crowd and heard the heated words directed at my mother, I ran over. When he saw me, the strongest brother rushed toward me, shouting at my mother, "Today, I'm going to make you heirless."

It was October. All the manure collected during the rainy season had been taken to the fields, so the compost pit next to our house was empty. One of those brothers pushed my mother aside, and another picked me up by the neck and threw me in the compost pit. The other three brothers came rushing to the pit with their bamboo sticks to beat me, but the bottom of the pit was so narrow that the sticks couldn't quite reach me. I lay there, motionless. Within a few minutes, some courageous people from the crowd, including the mother and sisters of the bullies, grabbed them and pulled them away. I climbed out of the pit, but immediately one of the brothers pushed through the crowd and threw me into the pit again. In a futile attempt to injure me, he began flailing at me with his bamboo stick. When the stick still did not reach me, a thought flashed in my mind: "The pit is narrow so they can't hurt me by swaying the stick, but they could very well poke me to death with the tip. Is it because of the commotion that they are not able to understand how to reach all the way down here?" Once again I climbed out of the pit, but in spite of the screaming, crying, and shouting of the crowd (which was now quite large), they caught hold of me and threw me back into the pit. They did this six more times.

The seventh time, while lying at the bottom of the pit, I began thinking, "There is no injury to my body. When I get out, they shout at my mother and at me, shake me a few times, and throw me in this pit again, but it always feels like I am falling into someone's lap. Why? Because the soil in the compost pit is so soft? They are intent on hurting me, so why can't they figure out how to poke me with the sharp end of the stick?"

Absorbed in these thoughts, I felt a tender touch of loving hands all over my body. I knew that I was surrounded by the protecting hands of the Divine. The tip of the bamboo and even the strong hands of those macho men could have injured me seriously, but they had not. "I should not be afraid of anyone," I said to myself as I climbed out of the pit for the last time. Just then my father arrived. He turned to the five brothers and said, "If a few yards of land makes you happy, have it. But for that, you did not have to hurt a child." Then he looked at me and said, "Take your bath and go to school."

I picked up my bucket, fetched water from the well, washed, ate some yogurt and rice, and set out for school. On the way, I thought, "Are humans any better than animals? Why do people waste their lives hurting others? The people here are petty and so foolish that they find joy in seeing others unhappy. I was born here, but I do not find a single reason to remain—there is no love, no school, no friends, no understanding of life, and no means of livelihood. My parents are misfits here. They are kind and generous. Why were they born in this era? Life is a mystery." By this time, I was a half mile away from my home. With deep sadness, I looked back toward my village, and with a firm decision, I bid good-bye to the land of my birth.

From then on, I lived at the Sanskrit school with my teachers, visiting home occasionally, but only for a few hours. I never spent another night there. My parents accepted my decision. They too left the village soon after I moved to Allahabad to attend the university.

There is a turning point in every individual's life, and during those moments, each of us is accompanied by divine protection and guidance. Every event, regardless of how bitter and unpleasant it may seem, is a direct expression of divine will and contains the seeds of higher good. How mysterious is the divine will that used bullies to throw me in a compost pit and then protected me from them with her tender and invisible hands? Without this incident, I might not have had a direct experience of her grace, and without that experience, my faith in the Divine Mother would have remained dormant—at least until the next turning point came.

An Emotional Fit

Life at Sanskrit school was austere but pleasant. I had only one little problem—I wished for a room of my own so I could do my daily meditation and recitation of the scriptures without distraction. I did not want to expose my practice to anyone, for I had seen how my father and my Sanskrit teacher held their practices sacred and did them secretly. One day, I figured out how to overcome this problem.

There was a big temple next to the school. It had five chambers, one of which housed the idol of the goddess Durga, my favorite form of the Divine Mother. One day, when I was visiting this chamber, a thought flashed in my mind: "I should do my meditation here in the dark hours of the early morning. By the time anyone else comes for worship, my practice will be over." From then on, every morning, in the dim light of the ceremonial lamp, I did my meditation and the recitation of the scripture. However, it wasn't long before the local landlord, whose ancestors had built this temple, found out about my routine. He investigated, and when he discovered that he knew my father, he convinced my Sanskrit teacher that my daily meal should come from his palace.

There was a little kitchen adjacent to the temple. An elderly lady brought the groceries and firewood from the palace. Her job was to clean the kitchen, do the dishes, prepare the ingredients, and make the fire. I cooked for myself. In those days, I maintained an ideal life of an orthodox brahmin: I ate food only if it was cooked by me or by others belonging to the brahmin class. After the meal was ready, I served it on a bronze plate, took it to the temple, and after offering it to God, ate alone. Whatever was left over went to the servant. I tried to cook only what

I could consume, but it was hard because the servant always cleaned and washed too much rice and beans, and she always prepared enough chapati dough for several people. After several requests, when I did not see any change in her work pattern, I started making only as many chapatis as I could eat, leaving the rest of the dough uncooked. She did not like this and expressed her displeasure by playing subtle mischief. For example, she started bringing wet firewood. She would make the fire with a few dry sticks and then depart, leaving me to deal with the endless smoke. No matter how long I blew on the fire, it never got hot enough to boil the rice. This continued for weeks. Not knowing what else to do I started skipping meals. I was too embarrassed to tell my teacher what was going on. I considered myself an adult and thought I should know how to manage my own life. Further, I did not want my elderly teacher to cook for me, and he wouldn't eat if I cooked for him.

One day, the servant brought all the groceries and some wet firewood. She dumped everything in the kitchen and left, saying there was an emergency at her home. It was rainy season and everything outside was wet. I started the fire with kerosene oil, but as soon as the kerosene was consumed, the fire died, leaving the wood untouched. I reasoned that if I kept pouring kerosene oil in small portions, then eventually the fire would catch. After doing this for an hour, I thought perhaps the flame of the kerosene oil had cooked the rice. With high hopes, I opened the lid and found that the water had not even boiled, and the rice was just lying untouched on the bottom of the pan. In my frustration, I wanted to pour the pot of rice on the floor and catch hold of the servant and beat her up. Somehow, I managed to keep my composure. My eyes were red from the smoke; hunger and the constant blowing on the fire was making my head spin. I told myself,

*Left: the temple
next to the
Sanskrit school*

*Below: the
kitchen behind
the temple*

61

"Even if this rice is not properly cooked, it doesn't matter. I am a young man, and on top of that, I'm hungry—I can digest it. God doesn't care whether the food being offered to him is perfectly done or not. As the scriptures say, love is the best offering that a human being can make, and all material objects are simply a token of one's love and faith."

I decided to consider the rice cooked, offer it to the Divine Mother, eat quickly, and go to class. I served the rice on my traditional bronze plate but when I saw the starchy water collecting toward the lower side of the plate, my head boiled with anger. My teeth clenched, and I began to shake. I sat there looking at my plate, and then at the earthen stove, and then at the firewood, and I thought, "Whom should I destroy?" I controlled myself with the thought that there was no point in being mad at anyone, and set off to take the plate to the altar.

The clouds outside were so heavy that the inside of the temple was darker than usual. I had accidentally left the rock that I used to make sandalwood paste in the middle of the inner chamber, and I tripped on it. When the starchy water splashed on the floor, I finally lost my temper. For a few seconds, I stood there, mindless, and then, overcome with rage, I threw the plate at the statue. It bounced off and clattered on the stone floor, making a sound so loud that it could be heard at the school. I walked out of the temple but I did not know where to go or what to do. Standing there in the rain, I realized my tantrum was not appropriate. This realization calmed me down a little bit, and I went back to clean up the mess.

Half-cooked rice was scattered everywhere. I had thrown the plate with so much force that some of the rice had lodged inside the attire of the various statues. Knowing it would take me hours to clean it up, I went to Guruji and said, "Guruji, there's a mess in the temple and I should clean it before anyone sees it."

He asked, "What mess?"

I said, "Rice and other kinds of things."

Guruji knew that there was something wrong. He gave me his permission to go and clean, but a few minutes later he came in quietly to observe, and being experienced, kind, and wise, knew what was behind it all. He left without saying a word.

Throwing a plate in God's face was clearly a spiritual offense. To cleanse me of this sin, my teacher gave the food he had already cooked for the day to the cows and quietly underwent a day-long fast in penance on my behalf. He asked other teachers to substitute for him and spent the day doing meditation and scripture recitation.

I was too embarrassed to visit him, but in the evening he prepared tapioca—a meal he ate only when he was fasting—and called me to join him for dinner. The two of us ate quietly.

After the meal, while massaging his feet, I whispered, "Guruji, I'm sorry. Please tell me, what are the consequences of making such mistakes?"

"It is not a mistake. It is called a fit of anger," he replied. "If you were small, it would have been called throwing a tantrum. But now you are an adult. If you don't learn to control yourself, you will have to clean up the messes you make. If you don't want to waste your life in cleaning up messes, you had better learn the art of acquiring a quiet mind."

I asked, "How can I learn that?"

He said, "Find the cause of the inner unrest that created this emotional turmoil. When you reflect on the subtle forces that caused you to lose your temper, you will find that unfulfilled desires are the cause of your anger.

"It is true that in her own way, the servant has been harassing you. She is ignorant. Like many other servants

working for these landlords, she has been earning her livelihood by stealing and manipulating. She knows that if she
takes uncooked groceries from the temple kitchen, she will
be punished for having taken too much from the palace
pantry—that's why she wanted you to cook more than you
could eat so she could carry the leftovers home. From now
on, there is no need of accepting anything from this landlord, but try to understand why this incident triggered your
anger. Definitely, the cause of the anger was already there.
The servant's behavior simply served as a spark."

That whole night, I contemplated on what my teacher
had said and realized that this inner unrest was caused by
my desire to have all the comforts and conveniences my
family once had. Throughout my childhood, I had heard
stories of my family's prosperity: hundreds of acres of
farmland, beautiful orchards, expensive jewelry, handmade
silk saris brocaded with gold and silver, and a household
attended by a score of servants. I grew up with tales
describing my father as the wisest and most respected
person in the region. In terms of generosity, my mother
had no equal. Yet through my own eyes, all I had seen was
poverty and humiliation. As I reflected more deeply, I saw
that from early childhood, I had felt that the economic
upheaval of my family was an unfair act of destiny, that
I had a right to inherit everything that my father had possessed when I was born—even though I had heard repeatedly from my father and others that whatever happens in
life is part of the divine plan, that divine will always pre-
vails, that divine will is always auspicious and good. Now
I realized that these words had only reached my head.
They had never sunk into my heart.

No More Priestly Business

My Sanskrit teacher was known for his piety, his knowledge of scriptures, and his skillful performance of rituals. Even though there were hundreds of pandits in the region who performed rituals for others, it was considered to be a great honor to have my Sanskrit teacher perform, or even supervise a ritual, so his services were always in great demand. Normally, he officiated at grand ritual ceremonies involving several pandits, and in these cases, his students carried out the ceremony under his supervision. At the end of the ceremony, the benefactor (the person sponsoring the ceremony) would give a love offering to my teacher, and he would share it with his students. But there were occasions when a ceremony was too long and too elaborate to be completed by the handful of pandits who had studied with him, and additional pandits had to be brought in. In these situations, everyone's duties had to be carefully defined.

On one such occasion, my teacher was invited to take charge of officiating at a grand ritual known as *sahasra chandi*, a ceremony that mainly involves reciting a scripture, consisting of seven hundred verses, one thousand times. In addition, there are hundreds of verses and mantras that must be recited before the thousand recitations begin and after it is completed. The *sahasra chandi* is an eleven-day group practice, and fifty pandits are required to complete it. Twenty came with my teacher and thirty from elsewhere. Thirty-three were assigned to do the actual recitation of the scripture, and the remaining seventeen made the preparations: gathering the ritual objects and arranging them properly, replenishing the ceremonial lamp with ghee, trimming the wick, washing the utensils, cooking and serving the food. It was understood that those who actually did the recitation were of higher rank than the others and were expected to maintain a higher degree of purity, which required that they observe stricter disciplines.

The ceremony began early in the morning. Even though I was the youngest of the pandits, my teacher assigned me the job of reciting the scripture. The benefactor took the ceremonial oath, officially accepting us as his priests. It took two hours to complete the preparatory steps. Then we began the recitation. Each of us in the group of thirty-three pandits was supposed to do three recitations a day. I had been reciting this scripture daily for the last three years and so I could do it by heart. I completed my first recitation in forty-five minutes and left the hall. I was very hungry but when I looked around and saw no sign of breakfast, I went back, did another recitation, and left the hall again, looking for food. This time, I told my teacher that I was starving. He asked the benefactor if there were any fruits or sweets I could snack on. When the benefactor replied that lunch would be ready soon, my teacher took a few raisins from the altar and gave them to me, telling me to eat them and to drink some water. Then I went back to my seat and did my third, and final, recitation of the day. After that I sat there reading the scripture to occupy my mind, but I was so hungry it was hard to concentrate. By noon, everyone else finished their first recitation, but lunch was not yet ready. We got our first meal of the day at two in the afternoon.

I told my teacher I had completed my three recitations and asked him what I should do in the afternoon. With a sparkle in his eyes, he said, "Let's do some studies," and we spent the afternoon on Sanskrit lessons just as we would have done at school. In the evening, I did not go to the ritual hall but instead I took care of my teacher:

fetching water for him, giving him a bath, drying his clothes, and massaging his feet after the evening meal. The next morning, I was ready earlier than the other pandits, and by the time I completed three recitations, the others were barely halfway through their first recitation. That day, my hunger pains were even more intense than the day before, but there was no cure for it. I had to wait until everyone else was done.

Most of these pandits had figured out where to get their morning tea and the sweets that people customarily eat when they fast. Officially, none of them had eaten, but they had all consumed a large amount of sugarcane juice before entering the hall. Once there, they spent hours performing rituals: preparing sandalwood paste, arranging utensils, sprinkling water, and driving away ants and bees who were drawn by the sweets that the pandits had left on their individual altars. Because they had consumed so much sugarcane juice, they had to get up for the bathroom frequently. The nature of the ceremony demanded that each time they used the bathroom, they had to perform an additional set of rituals: wash their feet and hands, rinse their mouth, change their ceremonial trousers, sprinkle sanctified water on the new set of clothes, and perform a portion of the preparatory practices all over again. I had never seen such a disorganized and sloppy way of performing rituals. And I could not understand why, in the middle of the rituals and recitation, they would look at each other, laugh, and make private remarks. Soon I discovered that most of those remarks centered around me.

Within a week, the air was filled with sarcastic jokes and comments: "Soon this young pandit is going to be a superstar," they would say. "When you are blessed by a guru, a scripture gets finished just because you look at it. When you have a super pandit like this young one, then in an attempt to go to heaven, the poor benefactor is bound to go to hell." Looking at my teacher, the pandits not trained by him would say, "Even a learned person becomes senile in old age."

Soon it was obvious that there was a division among the pandits, and that some of my teacher's students had joined the detractors. Even the benefactor was affected by this—he became extra generous in feeding me, and I knew that he was doing this so that I would not fake the recitation in order to escape my hunger pangs. I was deeply hurt.

My teacher continued his routine as usual, spending an hour each morning and evening in the ceremonial hall. The rest of the time, he taught me lessons, monitored the ceremony, provided spiritual guidance to those who visited him, or simply rested—all in a perfectly relaxed and peaceful manner. From his speech and behavior, it was impossible to tell if he knew how contaminated the atmosphere had become. However, on the seventh day, right before going to bed, he said something that churned the lake of my mind. Only after it settled down did I realize that he had infused it with wisdom that has served as a beacon of light to me ever since.

As I tucked my aged teacher into bed, he said, "There are many flaws and cracks in this ceremony, and I must see that it is completed with purity and precision. You love me; therefore I ask that in addition to the amount of practice you do during this ceremony, you give to the benefactor the fruits of one hundred recitations of this scripture that you had completed earlier. I will contribute one thousand. In this way, we'll perform this ceremony above and beyond the benefactor's expectation and leave these pandits to their own karmic consequences. I will teach you everything I know, but promise me that you will not throw pearls to swine."

The whole night, I tossed and turned, trying to understand how it is possible to give the fruits of your action to others, especially when it involves giving away spiritual benefits. My mind jumped from one question to another: As head pandit presiding over the ceremony, is my teacher responsible for completing it? What karmic consequences are the sloppy pandits going to face? Don't these pandits know that the successful completion of such practices requires that the participants maintain a positive mind and refrain from hatred, jealousy, and faultfinding? What did my teacher mean when he made me promise not to throw pearls to swine?

The next morning, I went to the ceremonial hall with my teacher. Making me hold sacred water in my hand and keeping the Goddess and nature's forces as witnesses, he read the *sankalpa* (ceremonial oath) and made me take a solemn vow to give away the benefits of one hundred recitations of the scripture. Then he did the same thing himself. After this, we continued as we had on previous days, except that in the afternoons, instead of grammar, he began teaching me the dynamics of rituals. What he taught me in those four days enabled me to understand the difference between ritualistic spiritual practices and ceremonial functions. During my last session, I asked what he meant by saying, "Do not throw pearls to swine."

"Be done with priestly business," he replied. "My wish is that after this practice is over, you will not take part in any such rituals."

"Then why did you teach me all this?" I asked.

"Because you are the custodian of the lineage of the sages," he answered. "Practice this for your personal growth. Keep the knowledge alive. Teach only those who are truly inspired and never teach those who intend to turn ritual practices into business. Do not officiate at rituals sponsored by benefactors who do not know the difference between religious ceremonies and spiritual practices. And even then, never, ever accept love offerings from anyone."

He continued, "The dark age is in full swing. Most

human beings are governed by greed and fear. Look at these pandits. Their minds are focused on name, fame, and money. They are using this ceremony as an opportunity to demonstrate their expertise: how much they know, how detail-oriented they are, how quick is their wit, how well they articulate the mantras. Ultimately they are demonstrating their organizing capacity and their communication skills—even though it is making them manipulate, lie, and criticize others."

Rituals are a valid path of spirituality, provided they are performed with full purity and precision. Ritual worship, in its own right, is a complete science, but today much of this science has been replaced by custom, dogma, and superstition. The efficacy of ritual practices is further diminished by the inner poverty of the priests who perform them with one intention—making money. Rituals are sacred. The indiscriminate display of rituals ruins their sanctity, and once the sanctity is gone, rituals become lifeless.

A Low-Grade Beggar

My Sanskrit teacher was fond of the holy city of Banaras and visited it frequently, taking me along. He stayed with his best friend, Agamachariji, one of the most learned pandits in Banaras. Agamachari lived a simple, pious, and disciplined life, and he was an unmatched Sanskrit scholar. He specialized in yoga and tantra and was a professor at the Sanskrit University's Department of Yoga-Tantra. As a professor, he was entitled to an apartment in the teachers' colony, but he preferred to live at an ancient temple, Dhoop Chandi, which had a few extra rooms for its caretakers. This particular temple, and the area around it, was beautiful and peaceful. Once inside the temple grounds, you wouldn't know that you were in one of India's most bustling cities. The temple was located at the edge of a small, deep pond that was filled only during the rainy season. The rest of the year, you could descend on stone steps twenty to thirty feet below the surface and enjoy the privacy of an underground cave covered by a canopy of limitless sky.

During my first visit to Banaras, this temple and its surroundings stole my heart. I stayed here with my teacher for four days, but we spent very little time at the temple because my teacher kept a busy schedule. He took me around and introduced me to his old friends and former colleagues. We bathed in the Ganga, worshipped Shiva at the main temple, visited endless sacred sights scattered throughout the city, met pandits specializing in various fields, and worshipped the Goddess at Annapurna, the famous Shakti temple. Only in the late evening hours did my teacher spend time with this learned scholar and holy man, Agamachari, and it was then that I got a glimpse of

Above: morning scene of the city of Banaras from the Ganga
Below: shrine of Batuka Bhairava in Banaras

the profundity of his academic knowledge, and his dedication to spiritual pursuits.

At first, I was overwhelmed. The feeling that I was not worthy to study with him made me timid, and so I remained in his presence only when my teacher was there. But soon I discovered that his kindness and humility exceeded even his scholarly knowledge and spiritual wisdom. At this realization, my hesitation vanished, and so whenever I did not need to be with my teacher, I joined Agamachari in his daily chores: fetching water from the well, watering his plants, sweeping the courtyard, and washing the stone floor of the temple. Thereafter, whenever I visited Banaras, with or without my teacher, I stayed at this temple, and there I received the same love and guidance as I did from my teacher.

Both my teacher and Agamachari were devotees of the Divine Mother. My teacher's method of meditating and worshipping the Goddess was simple. He followed the injunctions laid down in the scriptures belonging to the Vedic tradition. Agamachari's method was much more complex; he followed the meditative and ritual techniques as outlined in tantric texts, which meant that the spiritual path he followed was more mystical and esoteric than my teacher's. The more time I spent with him, the more I got involved in meditating on the Divine Mother in the tantric fashion.

My association with Agamachari also gave me access to the university's library, which had one of the best collections of Sanskrit scriptures and manuscripts. My association with Agamachari and access to the library widened my knowledge of scriptures and fueled my spiritual fervor, but distracted me from my coursework. I spent time traveling back and forth from Sanskrit school to Banaras, studying subjects with this great man that had nothing to do with my coursework, sitting in the temple or on the pond's steps doing my spiritual practices, and taking endless notes in the university's library. The result was that I barely passed my eleventh-grade exam in the summer of 1971.

The coming academic year filled my mind with fear and anxiety. My teachers couldn't believe that I had done so poorly on my exam; my friends were surprised; my parents were disappointed. I was so horrified by the idea of what might happen when it came time for final exams that I could not concentrate on my studies, nor could I do the meditation and scripture recitation that I had enjoyed for so many years. I had nightmares of arriving at the examination hall late and not being allowed to take the tests, of leaving my pen at home and finding that no one in the examination hall would lend me one, of having a pen that wouldn't work. And I kept remembering the prophecy of a palmist who had told my mother about my future when I was a child. The memory of that prophecy shook my conviction in myself and my faith in all the gods and goddesses.

This fortune-teller was a peddler and sold cookware in the village bazaar, but he was best known for his knowledge of astrology and palmistry. He carried merchandise on his bicycle and stopped at the doors of the villagers to sell his pots or trade the new for used ones, and to read people's palms and horoscopes free of charge. These peddlers normally avoided our home but one day when my father was away, one stopped by. My mother and women from the neighborhood gathered on our veranda, and he began reading people's palms. One of my distant aunts grabbed my hand and asked him to read my palm to see what was in store for me. He fixed his spectacles on his nose, rubbed my palm on his sleeves, stretched my fingers left and right, and began reading the fine lines of my palms: "*Bahu rani* [blessed young lady], how fortunate you are. This young boy is going to be a great man."

"What are the chances for his education?" my mother asked.

"Oh, *bahu rani*, in knowledge, he is going to exceed his father."

Then he pulled his spectacles down to the tip of his nose, stretched my palms open again, stared at the lines through his penetrating eyes, and spoke in a self-important voice, "He will study all the way to the eleventh grade, and his fame will spread throughout the land."

In a village where no one had gone beyond fifth grade, this prediction brought great joy to all those who heard it. But now, having barely passed my eleventh-grade exams, it stood before me like an invincible devil. I remember waking up every night with my lips dry, gasping for air. Even though I knew that this peddler used astrology and palmistry to entice his customers, I could not banish the memory of this "prophet" staring at my palms and predicting that I would study all the way to eleventh grade, so I poured all of my mind and heart into my studies. Since I could not sleep at night, I used my insomnia for doing japa and reciting scripture, with only one prayer: "Please help, help, help! I don't want to fail. I don't want to be doomed. I don't want to disappoint my parents. Don't let my life be in vain."

Sanskrit students were known for cheating on their exams so I befriended the most expert among the cheaters. They told me how to write answers on the thinnest paper, in the smallest letters, and tuck those notes in special pockets hidden inside my underwear. They taught me how to spray sugar syrup on those papers so the notes could be swallowed in an emergency. I had never in my life imagined that I would be preparing to pass my exams at the cost of cheating and killing my conscience. During the exam, I felt this devil of a prophecy standing before me, saying, "Boy, you are going to get caught red-handed, and that will be your end." I threw away the notes, telling myself, "Better to fail without this additional disgrace."

The exams went so well that I knew I would pass with high honors. Yet I could not banish the image of the village prophet holding his spectacles on the tip of his nose. After the exams were over, my Sanskrit teacher was busy performing wedding ceremonies and other rituals, so not knowing how to cope with my fear and anxiety, I went to Banaras and stayed with Agamachari. But this time, I had no desire to study with him or go to the library. Instead, hoping to win divine grace, I began an untiring pilgrimage to powerful shrines throughout the city that were known for fulfilling the desires of their devotees.

The exams of all the Sanskrit schools in the state were governed and monitored by the Sanskrit University of Banaras. In those days, the university registrar's office was notorious for its corruption. With very little money, you could bribe a clerk in the registrar's office to tell you who would be grading your tests, and then you could bribe the examiner. Many times I thought of going to the registrar's office and exploiting my connection with this great soul, Agamachari. Thank God each time I thought of doing this, a voice from deep within prevented me from committing a mistake for which I would never have been able to forgive myself.

Agamachari knew how restless I was, and yet he offered no help. One day, unable to contain my anxiety, I asked him, "Guruji, I am wondering who will be grading the exams?"

Without saying a word, he walked away. I was mortified—he knew why I asked that question. With a heavy heart, I went to the pond, sat on the last step above the water, and cried. I was so ashamed that I had no courage to show my face to him. But how long could I sit by the pond? Finally, when evening came, I went to the temple and found him seated on his cot. I placed my head at his feet, and apologized. In response, he said, "How has this weakness entered you?"

I told him the story of that palmist and put all my problems before him: fear, worry, anxiety, lack of self-trust, and my shaky faith in divine grace. When I had finished, he said with boundless love, "You cannot serve two masters. Either you can have trust in that palmist or trust in yourself. Either you can have faith in palmistry or faith in God. One who does not know who his creator is remains a victim of the unknown and calls it destiny. But one who knows who the creator is becomes fearless for he knows that the creator has deposited his creative force in his most beautiful creation—the human being. You are a repository of the creator's creativity. It doesn't befit you to live at the mercy of astrology and palmistry.

"It is not your desire to pass the exam but your doubt regarding passing it that made you pitiful. It has turned you into a beggar, one who is fortunate enough to meet the Queen of the Universe and yet so low that you beg her for a peanut. Rise above these petty desires. If you cannot, then replace them with higher desires. If you don't know what those higher desires are, then simply surrender, and let her decide what is best for you."

Agamachari's simple, powerful words drove away my confusion. My fear and doubt vanished and I returned to my normal self. A week later, the exam results came— I passed with high honors. At the advice of my Sanskrit teacher and Agamachari, I enrolled in the University of Allahabad.

Living *with* Grace

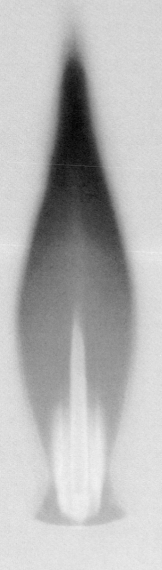

The Art of Adjustment

I spent the first nineteen years of my life in a world that prized simplicity, humility, and contentment. When I enrolled in the University of Allahabad, I left that world and entered one that cherished a set of values totally foreign to me. Patterned after Oxford, the University of Allahabad was one of the most prestigious educational institutions of India. For more than a century, its graduates occupied high-ranking positions in the British government and later in the democratic government of India. The majority of the faculty and students came from families who thought of themselves as aristocrats; they regarded my village values and lifestyle as old-fashioned and backward—even weird.

To be an acceptable member of the university community, you had to wear a shirt and trousers, preferably synthetic ones. You were "cool" if you wore bell-bottom trousers and a shirt with a long pointed collar. But it was expensive cigarettes, fancy sunglasses, pocket watches, and the ability to speak English that gave you access to the upper class. The more you knew about the personal lives of movie stars and politicians, the more progressive and informed you were thought to be. As one of the creators of a democratic and modern India, you had to eat in restau-

Senate Hall, the administrative building of the
University of Allahabad

rants once in a while, and by joining the table with people from all castes, you demonstrated that you had washed your hands of the orthodoxy of Hinduism. Since I had none of these virtues, I was a misfit.

It was the summer of 1972 when I first walked through the university gate wearing my traditional *dhoti* (a six-yard piece of unstitched fabric), *kurta* (tunic), and flip-flops—all in white—and my head clean-shaven except for a long ponytail that I combed and tied in a knot as part of my morning ritual. I went from building to building and window to window, inquiring where to obtain an application form, while people stared at me like a pack of dogs, alarmed and ready to deal with the albino wolf that had strayed into their midst. Obtaining an application form was an ordeal. I finally got the form, filled it out, and submitted it. After a couple of months, I received a card informing me that I had been accepted. Then the real drama began.

My first visit had already taught me a lesson: I had better learn the art of adjustment lest I be singled out. My father had once told me, "Life means adjustment. See, my son, I did not know how to adjust to a society that suddenly underwent a drastic change, and the result has been that society has no room for me. Adjustment means to find your place in society." Remembering this, I had used the two months between submitting the application and getting accepted into the university to acquaint myself with city life.

For untold ages, Allahabad had been one of India's greatest seats of learning. In sanctity, it exceeds all sacred sites of India, as is evident in its epithet, Tirtha Raja ("the Lord of all holy sites"). For more than a century, the British Empire used this city as the headquarters from which it ruled north and central India, and during that time, Allahabad embraced a form of Western culture that exerts its superiority over the native culture. The city became the center of political power, and as the influence of government officials, lawyers, judges, doctors, professors, politicians, and other aristocrats spread, the dignity of the traditional spiritual and educational institutions declined. The University of Allahabad was founded in 1858, just a year after the British took full control over all of India. To a large extent, the curriculum there, and at many other universities in India, was designed to produce graduates who could join the workforce of British India. Furthermore, simply because they lived in Allahabad, students of this university had the advantage of associating with those in power. Thus, from the day of their admission, most students considered themselves distinguished—a breed apart from the rest of the people of India. However, there were also those who held a balanced approach toward learning. They took full advantage of the Western system of education the university offered while retaining respect for their own culture, tradition, and values. Thus, in addition to producing officers in Indian civil services, attorneys, judges, and politicians, the University of Allahabad was known for graduates who emerged as India's greatest thinkers, philosophers, and reformers.

Considering how traditional my upbringing had been and how deeply rooted in orthodoxy I was, I had a long way to go in learning the art of adjusting myself to this atmosphere. In terms of food, dress, and lifestyle, adjustment came with ease. My diet, already simple, became even simpler. I mastered our famous village dish, *kichari:* boil rice, beans, vegetables, turmeric, and salt together, eat it, and be done. I replaced my traditional white outfit with a few pairs of colorful pants and some shirts. Instead of walking barefoot or wearing flip-flops, I adorned my feet with brand-name shoes, and I now had black hair on my head—the long ponytail was gone. As part of my daily routine, I still meditated and recited the scriptures, but while socializing with friends I threw about the names of politicians and actors and actresses, and talked about cars and motorcycles. In my jokes and expressions, I added some urban flavor. So far, so good. But the adjustment to the university's academic life always remained a challenge. I found the coursework shallow and stale—it was neither traditional nor contemporary. Most teachers simply regurgitated what was written in books—most often, in books that they themselves had written. In contrast to the intellectual stimulation of my Sanskrit school, the university education was boring and meaningless.

I had long dreamed of studying ancient texts in the light of modern thinking. Before coming to the university, I had imagined that I would be studying with those well versed in Eastern and Western streams of thought. Studying at their feet, I would discover the bridge between East and West, faith and reason, intuitive revelation and intellectual hypothesis, spiritual wisdom and worldly skills, and ultimately (I imagined) I would learn the art of creating a bridge between the sacred and the mundane in my own personal life. I joined the Departments of Sanskrit, Philosophy, and Hindi Literature with these high hopes, only to have them dashed in a few weeks.

The Sanskrit courses were the most disappointing of all. During my first four years of college, these courses covered only fragments of the texts I had already studied in-depth in Sanskrit school. Here at the university, all I was supposed to do was memorize the literal meaning of a few pages of those texts. It was like grammar school—just memorize what was required and then, during the exams, answer the questions in the language of the teacher. The slightest deviation from what the teacher had said would severely damage exam results. There was no room for discussion and analysis; there was no research or independent thinking. During their undergraduate- and master's-level studies, students were not required to write even one single paper. But I needed a piece of paper called a degree, so I had to go through the motions.

Courses in the Philosophy Department were somewhat more satisfying. Here, at least, I learned something new—Western philosophy and logic. But in the area of Indian philosophy, the curriculum was pathetic. Prior to entering the university, I had studied all the systems of Indian philosophy from the original sources. This traditional system of education had allowed me to discuss and debate the doctrines of different philosophers. I was trained to put myself in the shoes of each individual philosopher and reflect on the validity of his viewpoints. I was also trained to put myself in someone else's shoes and look at the same philosophy as an outsider, and then to put myself back in my own shoes and take an objective view. That, I was taught, was the way to arrive at a balanced stance. (This particular style of philosophical study is known as *uttara paksha* and *purva paksha*.) But here at the university, however, we did not delve into any original sources. Instead, we were expected to memorize what our classroom teachers said and wrote—without even bothering to see whether they had simply reworded the writings of others, or even if they had consulted the original texts of Indian philosophy.

During my first year of college, I worked very hard, even harder than I had the year before in Sanskrit school. When I took the exam, I thought that I had done well, but the results were disappointing. I learned the hard way— don't be precocious; simply be smart. Please your teachers and meet their expectations, no matter how low their expectations are. I concluded that the purpose of my higher education was not necessarily to learn anything about the meaning of life, but simply to get some degrees and cash them in for high-paying jobs, and search for meaning and purpose of life elsewhere.

The purpose of education is to unfold our dormant potentials, to help us become productive members of society, and to enable us to gather the tools and means to live happy, healthy, and joyful lives. But modern education is mainly geared toward developing the skills for earning money, for manufacturing, selling, and buying products, and for exploiting our innate desire for power and pleasure so that we can accumulate more and more worldly objects. I have yet to find a school where people can learn not only how to gather the objects of the world, but also to use them as tools and means to achieve true wealth—a healthy body and a joyful mind—and to further reinvest this wealth to find the meaning and purpose of life.

A Sinking Heart Begins to Soar

The poor grades I received in my first year at the University of Allahabad taught me a big lesson: don't be precocious, simply please your teachers and measure up to their expectations. I put this lesson into practice and the results of my next series of exams were excellent. My friends and teachers began to regard me as intelligent, but I knew that I was not sincere in my studies. I was putting hardly one-tenth of my heart into my studies, and I often wondered whether I was being dishonest with myself, deceiving my teachers, or bluffing the whole system of education. I also questioned whether getting a degree for the purpose of securing a high-paying job was really right. If money was the goal, I could get it without a university degree. I knew I could make good money by practicing astrology, palmistry, gemology, numerology, and esoteric rituals—expertise that had been passed on to me as part of my family tradition. But disenchantment with these very subjects was the main reason why I had come to the University of Allahabad.

Before coming to Allahabad, I had been imagining that a university education would help me find a decent livelihood, one that did not rely on practices which, in my observation, involved a great deal of hypocrisy, dishonesty, deception, and exploitation of human weaknesses. I had imagined that a university education would help me broaden my understanding of myself and of the world, and would help me create a world of my own in which I could live with dignity and peace. But once I was enrolled, I saw no sign that any of this would ever materialize. Rather, reality presented itself: memorize textbooks and get good grades, and then what? Become a teacher in one of these colleges and universities? Even if that were desirable, was it possible? Hundreds of scholars who had graduated years ago were still hanging around. They took a few courses now and then, not because they wanted to learn something new, but because their enrollment in the university allowed them to stay connected with the professors and university authorities. I saw many of these scholars spending their evenings at the homes of these authorities, trading university gossip and discussing politics to strengthen their relationships with them and to earn their favor, hoping it would come in handy one day.

I often wondered why I had come to this university. If I had not come here, where would I have gone? In those days, you had to have a connection with someone in power, particularly a politician, to get a good job; academic qualifications were secondary. I was a simple man from a village and had no connection with any bigwigs. All I had was knowledge of the scriptures, which had infused my heart with the conviction that simplicity, humility, and contentment are the fountains of true happiness. To establish a connection with someone with enough weight to push me into an academic position, I had to unlearn the virtues of simplicity and straightforwardness. I wondered if it was worth it.

I tried to envision my future. After a long analysis, I concluded that I had better prepare myself for government jobs that were solely dependent on standard tests, known as "competitions." But preparation for these competitions was an expensive affair, and my limited funds had already been exhausted. I could not bear to take money from my parents for my living and education expenses when I knew that they had already sold almost everything they owned—the farmland, orchard, cattle, and jewelry. The only way they could help me prepare for the competition to secure a government

job was to sell the remaining jewelry and perhaps their ancestral home. Squeezing the last drop of their sweat and
blood caused me to drown in utter dejection. I considered
dropping out of the university, but what else would I do?

Today when people come to me, asking, "I'm at
a crossroads—which way should I go?" I laugh and tell
them, "You are lucky that you are at a crossroads. In my
life, there were no roads. All the directions were so filled
with darkness that I couldn't see the space right in front of
my eyes, let alone discover the horizon."

During this dark period, one day I decided to visit that
great and kind soul, Agamachari, whom I had visited so
frequently when I was in Sanskrit school. When I got to
Banaras, I learned that this kind soul, who had guided me
in the past, was out of town. After leaving my blanket in
a corner of the temple, I went to see a saint named
Karpatri, who was believed to be an incarnation of Shiva.

I had known this swami since childhood. My father
had taken me to him on many occasions, as had my
Sanskrit teacher. Swamiji had such an overwhelming personality that only seekers of the highest caliber had the
courage to discuss spiritual matters with him, but he loved
me very much. In the past, he had always talked to me
about the Divine Mother, but this time, as soon as I arrived, he asked me about my future plans—study, career,
and so on. When I told him that I was preparing for a
competition to secure a government job, he laughed and
said sarcastically, "Sitting for a competition in order to get
a government job is good for those who do not have any
vision in life. It is a third-class person who competes for a
government job, and when a first-class person by chance
gets a government job, within a matter of a few months, he
turns into a third-class person." I was shocked to hear him
speak so bluntly.

He continued, "There is corruption in every government office. Often, a government employee who doesn't take part in the corruption is singled out and harassed by his colleagues. Many good, sincere, and honest government employees lose their jobs or end up in court because of false accusations. If they survive while living an honest life, then life for them is very hard because their salary is so small. On the other hand, those who take an active part in corruption make lots of money, but deep down in their hearts, they know they are corrupt, that they are thieves, and that they are hurting their country. Such people live with a heavy burden of guilt and self-condemnation. To overcome their guilt, they go to temples, they worship God, and give love offerings to swamis, gurus, pandits, and priests. But I know very well that no matter how much devotion they have for gods, goddesses, gurus, and holy men, their inner conflict and suffering never comes to an end. The dirty money they earn by creating pain for others is bound to pollute their minds as well as their family life. Sooner or later, their karma comes back to them: they betray their spouses; their spouses betray them; their children get into drugs and become loafers. I'm telling you, it is difficult to live a decent life while working in a government job."

I knew instantly that this great soul had read my mind; he knew exactly what was going on with me. "Swamiji," I replied, "I want to live a clean and peaceful life, but I do not know how to make it happen. I am not interested in teaching and perpetuating the lifeless system of Indian education, and if a government job is equally dissatisfying, then what is there for me to do?"

He said, "The truth is that there is no place for you in India. You are a thinker; you are a visionary. Today, Indian society does not have room to accommodate fresh ideas. It does not have respect for high visions and lofty ideals. Get out of India. Do that which makes sense to you. Become strong, and return to India only when you don't have to struggle to find your place in Indian society. Rather, come back only when you have unfolded your inner capacities and gathered the tools and means to create a place where not only you, but also many people like you, can be accommodated."

"Swamiji, I am not able to even manage my life in Allahabad," I argued. "I do not have the resources even to complete my education and you are telling me to get out of India. How is it possible? Where is the money to go abroad? And even if there is money, what will I do there? So far, all I know is how to recite scriptures."

"Why are you so discouraged?" he asked. "Do you want to be the creator of your destiny, or do you want to be a slave to your destiny? If you decide to be the creator of your destiny, God will help you. If you want to become the slave of your destiny, for that, too, God will help you. God's grace and the blessings of your ancestors will help you to do whatever you want to do and become whatever you wish to become."

At first this conversation only added to my confusion. But as time passed, it turned into a source of inspiration. The more I contemplated on it, the more it created self-trust, which eventually matured into a firm conviction: As a human being, I am blessed with infinite potential. With hard work and God's grace, I can do anything I wish. I knew that if I wanted to stay small, I would stay small. If I wanted to become big, I would become big, because the grace of the Divine Mother was always with me.

Live with Grace

When I left Banaras, I went to Amar Garh to visit my family. I had been away for some time and was shocked to see they were much worse off than I had imagined. A large portion of the house had collapsed during the monsoon, and my father's horse had died. He was already withdrawn, and the death of his horse fastened him further to his little village. To meet my college expenses, he had sold the only piece of farmland that was used for cash crops, such as potatoes and sugarcane. My parents were living hand to mouth. Yet they were determined to see that I completed my college education. I wanted to continue with my studies but my conscience would not allow me to put any more financial burden on them. Lying on my cot on the veranda the night before I left, I slipped into deep thought: "What a burdensome son I am. My parents could have gotten greater freedom from sorrow had I died at birth. Have I been anything more than a burden to my mother's womb? Am I not like that pony whose mother continues to work as a beast of burden, while her healthy adult son searches for an ideal and meaningful life?"

The next day, before I left for Allahabad, my mother gave me fifty rupees (in those days, this was equivalent to approximately ten dollars) and assured me that in the next couple of months, after the rice was harvested, she would send more money. My little sister told me secretly that my mother had been working hard for weeks to secure this money as a loan against future rice crops.

Drowning in dejection and self-pity, I took the money from her hand and went to see my father. He was in the middle of his morning meditation and scripture recitation. I stood at the door and waited until he reached the end of the chapter. Then he took a sip of the sanctified water and looked at me, signaling that now it was time to talk to him. I bowed my head and touched his feet. When he looked into my eyes, I could see the sadness there. When I asked what was the matter, he said softly, "Education is the best gift that a loving and dutiful father can give to his children. There was a time when I was able to give this gift to many children. I don't know what bad karmas I have done in my past that today I am not able to fulfill my fatherly duty."

Drops of tears rolled down his cheeks. I knew that if I stayed another second, I would crash. "No, no, Father!" I exclaimed. "Don't worry. Once I reach Allahabad, everything will be fine. Last year's scholarship is about to be released." And I sped out of the room.

I loved my sisters very much and had never left home without saying a million good-byes to them. They always chased me at least a quarter mile and turned for home only when I could convince them that I would return home soon. Today I feared that our love for each other might make me weak, and I went out the back of the house so that my sisters would not see me leaving.

The bus stand was almost a mile from our home. I got there, climbed on the bus, and, not wanting to see or talk to anyone, closed my eyes, pretending to be asleep. The bus rolled along the bumpy, winding dirt road, shaking all the limbs and organs of the passengers. As we bounced along, turbulent thoughts and emotions began to churn the lake of my mind: "Are humans any better than other creatures? Like them, we are born and grow, only to die one day. How lucky animals are—they spend their time eating, sleeping, procreating, and coping with survival. Their fear and anxiety is short-lived. Guided by nature, they embrace death without much fuss. But how miserable we humans are! How helplessly we are born, how helpless is our infancy, how we struggle as adults, how heavy is the burden of fear and anxiety when we grow old, how helplessly we die. This misery is made worse when we try to find meaning and purpose in life instead of accepting it as it is."

These thoughts were mixed with memories—the loving kindness of my mother, the wisdom of my father, the affection of my sisters, the selflessness of the teachers at the Sanskrit school. I remembered my latest encounter in Banaras with the great saint Karpatriji, and how, just a few days earlier, he had infused my heart with the noble idea that it was totally up to me whether I wanted to be the creator of my destiny or a slave to it. Then another thought would come: "These are just lofty ideas—they help you build your ambitions. Many people go on chasing their ambitions only to be disappointed when they reach nowhere."

With these thoughts churning in my mind, I reached the midpoint on my journey to Allahabad and switched from the bus to the train. The train ride was much smoother than the journey by bus. The currents and undercurrents in the lake of my mind, too, had become calmer. I was still sad, but my despondency had softened into dispassion. The complaining tone of my inner dialogue was turning into prayer, and I was able to remember the stories of many aspirants who were more miserable than I was, yet at some point in life were blessed with inner guidance and divine protection. All those stories said that you receive inner guidance and divine protection from the realm beyond only when you turn your face from this world. A strong thought arose: "Leave this world behind. Seek divine protection." This was swiftly followed by another thought: "If I vanish, what will happen to my parents? They are getting old. They will die of grief. What will happen to my sisters? They, too, will suffer their whole lives." Then I thought, "This type of thinking itself is an act of maya, delusion. No one suffers on account of anyone. Time is the greatest of all healers. Many adult sons die and their elderly parents go on living."

Just a few miles before the train reached Allahabad, I remembered stories about sadhus who, in search of divine guidance, walked upstream along the bank of the Ganga, and before reaching its source in the Himalayas, they received that which they were seeking. So just before the train stopped at Prayag Station in Allahabad, I decided that I would live with grace or not at all. "A dead life is not for me," I thought. "To shine even for a flash is better than smoldering through a long, weary life. No more college. No more emotional ties with anyone. I'll walk along the bank of the Ganga. I will not accept anyone's generosity. I will drink Ganga's water. I will walk close to the river, so if I collapse, I will fall into her and die in her lap."

As soon as the train stopped at the station, a host of beggars swarmed around it. I still had more than forty rupees and I started giving the bills to the beggars in amounts perhaps they had never imagined. They thought that I was a rich man, so they followed me until I gave them my little nylon bag containing my shirt and pajamas. A few beggars followed me further, but when I took off my shirt and threw it toward them while walking swiftly away, they concluded I was insane rather than rich and stopped following me. I walked to the bank of the Ganga under the Fafamau Bridge and started following the river upstream.

After about a mile it became too dark to go any farther, so I spent the night under a banyan tree. It was cloudy and dark and a chill wind fanned the fire in my tummy. To keep my mind off hunger and cold, I kept remembering the mantra that my Sanskrit teacher had given me long ago. At sunrise, I resumed my journey upstream.

I had hardly walked ten minutes when I saw some

cement steps leading up to an ashram. There, under a big pipal tree sat a thin, radiant saint on his wooden cot. Seeing this saint from a distance, a saying began to ring in my head: The virtue of a moment's meeting with a true saint far exceeds the virtues of all seven heavens combined, provided your visit to the saint is not motivated by ego and attachment. I made up my mind: "Let me visit this saint. I will not ask him for anything."

It was a small ashram and the sadhu was sitting quietly by himself. I put my head at his feet. He opened his half-closed eyes, looked at me, and asked, "Who are you?"

"I am one of the most helpless, aimless, and pitiful students of Allahabad University," I replied. "My name is Rajmani Tigunait."

The saint said, "The Lord of Life is the highest power of protection and guidance. It is in the Lord of Life the wise ones seek to find everlasting protection. Take refuge in that Divine Being. Upon knowing that Great One, whatever you desire will be yours."

"How do you come to know about that Great One?" I asked.

The saint replied, "It can be known only through a guru, a realized master."

"Who is a guru, and how do we recognize him?" I asked.

"No one is anyone's guru and no one is anyone's disciple," he replied. "The merciful Mother alone is the guru. Moved by her intrinsic compassion, she appears before her child in the form of a guru."

At this, I did not know what else to ask. If she herself is the guru, I thought, then finding a true guru, a realized master, is as difficult as finding the Lord of Life, the Divine Mother herself. Meanwhile, the saint picked up his slate and chalk, drew a geometrical design, and then handed the slate to me, saying, "Can you draw it?" Without waiting for my response, he picked up his water vessel and walked away toward the river. While he was gone, I looked at this geometrical pattern and tried to copy it on the other side of the slate. When he returned I handed the slate to him. He looked at what I had drawn and asked, "How did you draw it?"

I took the slate from his hand, erased my drawing, and drew it again. When I handed the slate to him, he took it, and with a profound reverence, bowed his head to the drawing and said, "The manner in which I drew it is meant for monks and renunciates, but the way you drew it is meant for students and householders." Then he stared into my eyes for a few moments and spoke lovingly and yet firmly, "No need of walking on the bank of the holy Ganga. Go back home. No matter where you are, from now on, the Divine Mother will be there in one form or another, ready to provide you with all you need."

I was awestruck; there was no doubt this great soul knew what was going on with me. The geometrical design he had drawn on the slate, and the way he explained the subtle distinction between the two different ways of drawing it, confirmed that he was a master with profound wisdom. I had seen that geometrical design before. In the tantric tradition, it is called Sri Chakra, and according to tantric adepts, meditation on it is the highest form of spiritual practice. I had read about it, and my father and my Sanskrit teacher had taught me about it, but all of these sources stressed that I must not practice it unless I was officially initiated by a competent master. The prospect of being initiated into this practice thrilled me, and yet I did not want to be deterred from my decision not to stop my journey until I had reached the goal of living with grace or not at all.

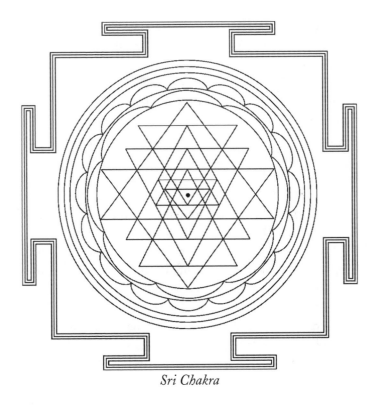

Sri Chakra

While he was trying to convince me that I had already received the gift of her grace and that all I needed was to cultivate sensitivity to experience her presence, one of his students walked up. The saint asked the student to bring some fruits, and while I ate the apples and bananas he went into his hut and brought out a shawl and a pair of flip-flops. He handed these items to me along with a ten-rupee bill and told me in a commanding voice, "Go back home. Do not dishonor her grace by ignoring my advice. You have a family, don't you? They must be worried. Tell your parents what transpired today and then join your school as guided by her."

I no longer had any doubt. I was sure that the Divine Mother had walked into my life in the flesh in the form of this saint. I had no idea how the future would unfold, but I knew that it would. I took his advice as the Divine Mother's command and returned home. This saint turned out to be one of the greatest architects of my life. What I received from this great soul is a treasure that I wish I could share with the seekers of divine grace as lovingly and selflessly as he shared it with me. The name of this great soul is Swami Sadananda.

The Past Returns

Following Swami Sadananda's instructions, I returned home and spent the night with my parents and told them about my meeting with Swami Sadananda. They had no idea who this swami was, but to them, all saints were venerable souls, so even though I did not say much about the discussion that had taken place, they accepted this meeting as God's will.

The next day, as I was getting ready to go back to Allahabad, I saw a car pulling off the dirt road onto the shoulder; a dignified gentleman in his early forties got out of the car and began walking toward our house. From the back seat two ladies—one quite elderly—emerged with grace and dignity. When my father saw this man approaching he looked at him with disbelief. Then suddenly, he jumped up from his cot and the two men embraced each other with tears in their eyes. I had never seen my father so overcome with emotion. Meanwhile, the elderly lady walked up and put her arm around me, and said with an outpouring of joy, "*Bete* [son], you have become so big!" My mother arrived on the scene and now all the ladies hugged each other. Then my mother turned to me and said, "He is Anand Bhaiya. She is Baraki Amma, his mother, and she is Bahu Rani, his wife. Pay your regards to them."

I had been hearing about this family since early childhood. This man my parents called Anand Bhaiya was Anand Pratap Singh, the eldest son of one of the north Indian landlords. His father had been the prime minister of the state of Amar Garh, where my father had been the royal teacher. My father and Anand Pratap Singh were like twin brothers—my grandmother had nursed both infants and they had passed their childhood together. I knew my father had a profound love for Anand Pratap Singh. As children, Anand and my father used to chase each other like dogs and cats. My father liked to bark like a dog so the elderly people in both families called him Bhukku ("the one who barks like a dog"). When the landlordship was abolished in 1952, this family left the village and this was the first time our two families had seen each other in twenty years.

While my mother busied herself making the guests feel at home, my father and Anand Pratap Singh exchanged their affectionate complaints:

"You totally forgot me."

"You have no heart."

"Did you drive this way by mistake?"

Then my father asked, "Where have you been all these years, and what are you doing now?" Both briefed each other about their "lost years." Anand Pratap Singh told my father that for the past several years he had been the personal assistant to Maharaja Dinesh Singh. This gentleman had been a member of parliament since independence in 1947 and had also held a cabinet-level portfolio in the government of India for the past twenty-five years.

Meanwhile Anand Pratap's mother was taking inventory of our family affairs: how many children my parents had, how old we were, which school we went to, and so on. When she learned that I was enrolled in the university and had been living in Allahabad for the last year, she said, "What is this nonsense? Under our noses my son is living like an orphan! Didn't you people ever tell him that he has a home in Allahabad?" Then looking at me, she said, "Your father has always been like this. You come with us." Addressing my father by his childhood nickname, she said, "Bhukku, will you ever change? I'm taking Rajmani with me! You just be quiet." Upon hearing this nickname, both my father and Anand Pratap Singh once again embraced each other and wept.

These forgotten members of my father's "past" family spent a few hours at our home, and after lunch they drove me to their home in Allahabad, and there I stayed during the rest of my years at college. Even to this day, I continue to receive the same love and affection from this family as I receive from my own. Meeting with them gave me access to a whole new world—a world that afforded me the opportunity to experience the Divine Mother's grace in all situations and circumstances, for this meeting eventually led me to my master, Sri Swami Rama.

How Grace Works

In late 1973, I moved to Anand Pratap Singh's house in Allahabad. He himself lived in Delhi with his wife and children, but his extended family—mother, uncles, aunts, sisters, and nephews—all lived in his house in Allahabad. His mother and the rest of the family took me under their wing. Now I had all the love and protection that I needed to live a comfortable and peaceful life. Within a matter of a few days, Anand Pratap Singh gave me a VIP tour of the city and introduced me to high-ranking personalities like the advocate general of India, the vice-chancellor of the university, the governor of the state, Mrs. S. S. Nehru (aunt of the prime minister, Indira Gandhi), and the group that coalesced around such people. All of this happened in less than a week. These new developments brought a great sense of security and stability, but the chain of events happened so fast that it seemed like a dream.

As soon as I could, I visited Swami Sadananda, the saint who, just a few weeks earlier, had told me, "No need of walking on the bank of the holy Ganga . . . from now on, the Divine Mother will be there in one form or another, ready to provide you with all you need." After paying my regards when I sat at his feet, he asked, "So, how are you now? Has the relationship between you and her improved, or are you still mad at her?"

I could not speak. I simply put my head at his feet. A moment later, he spoke again, "Remember, the grace of the Divine is pouring in all the time. Because we do not know it, we suffer from inner poverty. Inner poverty causes despair in the external world."

"Swamiji," I asked, "how does this grace work? How did Anand Pratap Singh suddenly remember his birthplace?

Who brought him there?"

Swami Sadananda replied, "The one who brought you here brought Anand Pratap Singh there. The Lord of Life is all-pervading. The Divine Being is our inner and eternal friend. Seated in the cave of our hearts, she watches over us. No one is ever helpless, for her loving and protecting arms reach every nook and cranny of the universe."

"I understand, Swamiji," I argued, "but why did I have to go through all this turmoil?"

Swami Sadananda explained, "Before the actual drama starts, so much goes into setting up the stage. Unless the stage is set, the conclusion will not have any impact."

"Swamiji, I don't understand."

"You don't need to understand everything today," he answered. "You have some understanding now. When the right time comes, you'll get the rest. But tell me, do you practice *gayatri* mantra?"

"Whatever little I know about *gayatri*, on that basis I practice," I replied.

He asked me to repeat the mantra and when I did, he said, "A seeker desirous of freedom from all forms of bondage should practice the *gayatri* mantra accompanied by five *Oms*. When the right time comes, I'll initiate you into this form of *gayatri* mantra."

This conversation led me to realize that as important as it is to work hard, it is even more important to remember that the divine will supersedes all human endeavors. There is a time for everything. The Divine Force has its own way of arranging the stage and performs its wonders only when the time is ripe.

chapter three

The Power of Prayer

While living in Allahabad, I spent a great deal of time with Swami Sadananda. As time passed, I realized he had profound knowledge of many fields of learning. He was an expert palmist, astrologer, philosopher, and Sanskritist as well as an accomplished healer. People from all levels of society came seeking a cure for various diseases, and he often gave them medicines he had prepared with the help of his students. Several times I asked him to teach me something about medicine, but he consistently refused. I asked him for medicine a few times when I was sick, but he ignored me. I could not understand this. Then one day, I received news that my mother, still living in the village, had been having terrible headaches for more than a month and had recently lost her eyesight. I made plans to go home and bring her to the city for treatment. Before I left, I went to Swami Sadananda and begged him to give me some medicine for her. "Medicine can help," he replied, "but it will take too long for her to get cured."

"Then, Swamiji, what can we do to help her get rid of her headaches and regain her eyesight?"

"Physical medicines are only one way of curing a disease," he replied, "and in fact, such medicines are too weak to change the course of karma, which is actually the root cause of any disease. Forget about such weak medicine. It will be better if you do the recitation of a special set of prayers dedicated to the Sun." Thus he gave me a prayer known as *aditya hridayam* from one of the scriptures.

Although I did not understand, I did the practice because I had faith in Swamiji. I did not go home, but stayed in Allahabad. The recitation took only an hour or so every day so I continued my studies at the university. After twelve days passed, I received a letter from my sister saying that my mother had suddenly recovered.

Deeply grateful, and curious about the relationship between the prayer and my mother's recovery, I went to see Swami Sadananda and asked him, "Swamiji, how can prayer help not only the practitioner, but also someone at a distance?"

He replied, "Intense austerity, intense meditation, recitation of mantra, grace of God, selfless service, and living in the company of saints create a powerful, positive karma in a short period of time. The energy created by spiritually vibrant actions can neutralize the effect of previous negative karmas. If karmas cannot be changed or modified, then why should anyone bother to do anything good in life?"

I asked, "Is it that karmas created by these kinds of practices neutralize our negative karmas, or is it the grace of the Divine that erases our negative karmas?"

Swamiji replied, "In my opinion, repetition of mantra, charity, company of good souls, prayer, and austerity help you eliminate your karmic impurities. Once the inner impurities are gone, you are able to receive and retain the grace of the Divine. Grace is the true source of the healing force, but the purification is what enables you to become a conduit through which grace can flow.

chapter three

Serving Nature

One Sunday morning, I found Swami Sadananda on his cot under the pipal tree. In front of him sat a gentleman who suffered from epileptic fits so violent and frequent that someone always accompanied him to make sure he didn't hurt himself.

When I arrived, Swamiji was in the middle of explaining to the patient that the medicine he was about to give him was quite potent. Then, handing him a substance that, to me, looked like ash, he said, "Take this medicine every morning, but only after you have fed grains to wild birds. After your morning ablutions, get some barley, cracked wheat, and other grains. Invite the birds to come to you and feed them. Once they have eaten, take this medicine. Only then may you take your meal."

When the patient and his attendant left, I said, "Swamiji, I understand the value of taking medicine, but why does he have to feed the birds?"

"You should watch," Swamiji replied. "When he is cured, I'll explain."

For three days, the poor fellow starved because the birds would not eat the grain he scattered for them. Then on the fourth day, they accepted his offerings, and he started taking the medicine. It became his routine to feed the birds before starting his day. In a month, his fits came less frequently; within six months, he was cured.

When I asked Swami Sadananda to explain, he said, "Birds are part of nature. Their relationship with humans is not contaminated with selfishness and expectations. They are happy when you serve them, but they do not mind if you don't. They operate on instinct alone—they make no personal choices and have no agendas. Serving

108

them is serving nature. Nature is the repository of all of our karmas, the impressions of our past deeds.

"In our unconscious mind," he continued, "we have the seeds of disease as well as its cure. This unconscious mind always works in conformity with nature. By nature, I don't mean only plants, rivers, and the rest of the natural environment. What we call nature, in fact, encompasses an entire primordial energy field that is the source of, and locus for, this material world. Everything and everyone evolves from this primordial energy field, including our natural world.

"By sacrificing your comforts, and giving away that which you believe to be yours, you pay off your karmic debts in the subtle realm. And it is these karmic debts that are the cause of our present misery. Although we do not have access to our own unconscious mind, we can still pay off our karmic debts by serving nature, of which we are a part."

CHAPTER FOUR

Miracles
and Mysticism

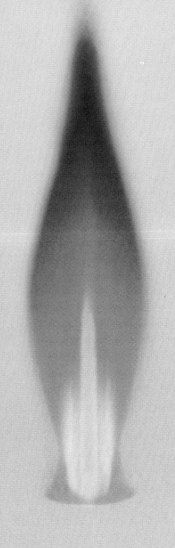

Changing the Course of Destiny

I had the good fortune to study with another swami, Swami Krishnananda. He was a wandering sadhu, but he spent the months of January and February in Allahabad. Every twelve years a great spiritual festival, the Kumbha Mela, attracts millions of people from India and abroad. It is celebrated on the banks of the Ganga outside the city of Allahabad for a month in the winter. During the other eleven years, crowds of pilgrims, saints, and religious leaders from various traditions gather here to celebrate a month-long festival called Magh Mela.

One winter, Swami Krishnananda was camped on the bank of the Ganga during the Magh Mela with a group of his followers. A healthy young man from one of the eastern states of India came to visit this saint. For no apparent reason, this young man had become obsessed with the thought that he would soon meet with a fatal accident. After listening to his problem, Swamiji instructed the young man to stay with him for a while at his campsite on the riverbank.

After a few days, the young man became impatient. Early one morning, he decided to take the next train home. Swami Krishnananda strongly advised him not to go, but the young man argued that he needed to get back to his job. The saint pleaded, "You know, I have become old. These days, I am not feeling well. Here everyone is busy doing spiritual practices, and no one is taking care of me. I need some medicine from the town, and due to the heavy crowds, the mela authorities have put a ban on vehicles. You are a young man; you can walk a few miles. You are the only one who can bring my medicine to me."

The young man still insisted on going. The saint said, "Life is short. I don't know whether or not we'll meet again. You have done so much for me these past few days. Why don't you do this one final service for me?"

The young man agreed. He went to the town and got the medicine, but in the process, he missed his morning train. The next day brought news that the train had been wrecked, killing more than one hundred passengers and injuring several hundred more. The young man, overwhelmed with gratitude, now wanted to stay and serve the saint, but the holy man insisted that he go home.

One day, in the course of conversation, I asked Swami Krishnananda if he knew the train accident would happen. He said, "No, however, for no apparent reason, I was not comfortable with him leaving. The voice of my heart told me he must stay here. I simply listened to the voice of my heart. I knew that this voice could not be wrong, so I created this drama."

A person with a pure heart is spontaneously and effortlessly in touch with the Divine within. This inner connection and the purity of his heart allows unconditional love to flow through him. Love supersedes regular laws of nature, including the law of karma that propels the wheel of destiny.

The Science of Spirituality

Swami Sadananda was known for his profound knowledge as well as for his healing powers and miraculous deeds. Even though more than a quarter of a century has passed since he left his body, people in Allahabad still remember him for his extraordinary knowledge of botany, alchemy, yoga, tantra, and ayurveda. Professors, judges, attorneys, and other educated people who were initially skeptical became his students once they gained direct experience from the practices they learned from him.

Many stories about Swami Sadananda have now become legend. For example, once two adversaries took their case to court. As is normal in the Indian judiciary system, the hearings were postponed repeatedly, and the case lingered on and on. The animosity between the litigants intensified, and finally one party came to Swamiji, seeking his blessings for winning the case. Swamiji replied flatly, "I don't have such blessings. I can teach you a special practice that will make you invincible, but I can't guarantee that you will defeat your opponent."

The man begged for the practice, and eventually, Swamiji taught it to him. It was a tantric practice known as *aparajita vidya* ("the knowledge pertaining to the Invincible One"). Swamiji also taught the man several complementary practices and how to arrange them around the main practice. Swami Sadananda then instructed the man to complete the whole course of meditation on a specific mantra while sitting under the canopy of the aparajita plant *(Clitonia ternatea)* which was growing at his home. After the practice was completed, Swamiji guided this man in how to make a paste out of the root, stem, leaf, flower, and fruit of the same plant. Then he helped him

115

imbue the paste with the power of the mantra. The next day, he instructed the man to put a dot of this paste on his forehead before he went to meet his opponent in court. Swami Sadananda predicted, "He will become your friend as soon as he sees you. He will drop the case voluntarily. But you must promise that you will treat him as your friend and not hold on to your animosity."

As the parties were entering the courtroom for the hearing, they looked at each other and their animosity vanished. The legal counsel for the opponent was shocked when his client told him he wanted to drop the case.

When I heard about this, I asked Swamiji, "Since you have this knowledge, why don't you help others who are also in court?"

"I did it as an experiment to show you people that these sciences are valid," he replied, "but as far as the case is concerned, it is not fully resolved—only postponed. These men will have to work out their karma sooner or later. Nothing other than knowledge and non-attachment can burn the karmic seeds and destroy the animosity between these two once and for all."

Spirituality is a complete science in its own right. It carries an overtone of mystery only for those who do not understand the interconnectedness of all aspects of creation. Humanity could benefit from this science immensely, provided it is studied and practiced systematically. Just as with any science, spirituality has its unique language consisting of specialized terminology and expressions. Re-discovery of this science requires that we commit ourselves to in-depth study, research, and experiments.

The Power of Mantra

One evening when I visited Swami Sadananda, I found his ashram unusually quiet. He was sitting on his wooden cot under the tree by himself. Despite the natural quietude that always surrounded him, he was in a jolly mood. I did not want to disturb his peace, but as soon as I offered my respect and sat before him, he said with a chuckle, "People come here with all kinds of questions. You are the only one who has no questions for me."

"The love and guidance that you have given me so generously has taken care of all of my questions. But still, I have a great deal of curiosity," I said.

"What is that curiosity?"

"What is the source of miracles? How do miracles work? You are a treasure-house of miracles—I wish I could learn something from you."

"Be more precise," Swamiji said. "Tell me, exactly what kind of miracle do you want to see and learn?"

"Especially that which pertains to spiritual healing," I said.

Swamiji answered, "I can teach you. There are techniques that can be used for a quick fix. Practicing such techniques does not require too much preparation. However, they require that you are disciplined and that you follow the instructions without the slightest deviation. But remember, healing performed through such techniques does not address the main cause. What you see as a spiritual cure is simply momentary relief.

"There is another form of healing that requires a great deal of preparation. Inner purification is at the core of that preparation. Coming in touch with the divine will is the prerequisite for practicing this higher form of spiritual healing. In this form of healing, the healer himself is the first recipient of the fruits of his practice. The healing force spontaneously flows from him. His selfless love carries the healing force to all those around him. It takes very little time to learn but a long time to practice. So tell me, which kind of healing do you want to learn?"

I said, "Swamiji, first, please teach me the quick one. Once I see its result and how it works, I will have a greater motivation to learn something higher."

Swamiji said, "I'll teach you, but promise that you will not misuse it—that you will not use it to earn money and that you will not show off."

I gave my promise. He continued, "A long time ago, I went on an extensive pilgrimage. I traveled throughout India, the Himalayan kingdoms, and Tibet, all the way to the Middle Eastern countries. Returning from Mecca and Medina, I was passing through Sindh, which is now part of Pakistan. There, I met a *fakir* [mystic]. For a few days I stayed with him. When I was leaving, he passed on a healing mantra to me, along with instructions for how to practice it. Today, I am going to pass on the same mantra to you. From now on, it will become yours." With this, he closed his eyes for a few moments, and then whispered a mantra in my right ear.

The mantra was in Hindi. It included the names of gods, goddesses, saints, and mystics from both the Hindu and Islamic pantheon. Since the mantra was in Hindi, I understood its meaning. At first, I found both the mantra and its meaning bizarre. But because I respected Swamiji and had full faith in him, I accepted this long piece of prose as a mantra. Swamiji explained how to assimilate the power of the mantra into my psyche. This assimilation procedure, too, sounded bizarre. He told me to memorize the mantra and to go to the cremation ground during the next lunar eclipse, fix my seat, sit in a cross-legged position, and recite the mantra for as long as the eclipse lasted. Once I started the practice, I must not get up. That's what I did.

Not too far away from Swamiji's ashram, there was a cremation ground. Cremation grounds in India are normally located in desolate places, such as on riverbanks or at the outskirts of human settlements. Even today, you may find jackals and wild dogs roaming around these grounds at night. These places are said to be the abode of ghosts, spirits, and goblins. The cremation ground I chose was no exception.

I selected the spot in the light of day. Then, with flashlight, incense, and matchstick in hand, I arrived at the spot almost an hour before the eclipse started. It was late at night. As instructed by Swamiji, I drew a protective line around my seat with proper rituals. When the time came, I burned incense and began the recitation of the mantra. During the practice, I heard strange sounds that I attributed to the howling of distant jackals. I also saw some images appearing here and there. I told myself that I must be hallucinating. I concluded the practice with disappointment. I had been hoping that I would have an unusual or startling experience. "All I experienced," I said to myself, "was the howling of jackals and some images appearing in my mind due to the fear of being in a lonely place." The next day, when I told Swamiji about my uneventful practice, he assured me that I had assimilated the power of the mantra, and that it would definitely work whenever I used it.

Two years passed, and I almost forgot that I had ever done this practice. Then, one day during the month-long Magh Mela on the banks of the Ganga, I visited a holy man. The next day was a special bathing day and his campsite was full of pilgrims. Among them was a farmer from a nearby village who planned to spend the night at this holy man's camp, take a bath early in the morning, and leave before the crowds pushed in. But by the time he arrived at the camp, he had fallen sick. The holy man learned that, due to sickness, this pilgrim could not eat his dinner. So in the late evening, the holy man sent a servant to this pilgrim with a glass of milk. The servant returned with the undelivered milk, informing the saint that the gentleman was possessed. By chance, I was present when the servant returned with the news that the pilgrim was possessed. I had never seen a possessed person. I wanted to see how such a person looked, so I quietly walked out of the saint's tent and went to find the pilgrim.

By the time I reached him, it had turned into a real scene. His face was red, his eyes bloodshot, and he was rocking violently. From time to time, his whole body rose three to four feet in the air and then dropped to the ground with a thud. The poor fellow was bruised all over. A score of people stood around him, watching and making remarks to each other. Suddenly, I remembered the mantra I had practiced at the cremation ground. This was the perfect time to test it. I recited the mantra in my mind. In the middle of this long, prose-like mantra, there was a blank space. I was supposed to fill this blank space with the phrase requesting the mantric energy to heal the person the way I wished. As soon as I did that, the pilgrim returned to normal, although he was still feeling very weak.

Right in front of my eyes, this man was healed. But a sense of disbelief lingered in my mind. I thought, "Is this fellow faking? If he was healed because of what I did, then I should have felt something happening within me, or at least around me." Absorbed in my reasoning, I stood there for a few moments. Then I thought, "Well, let me repeat the mantra, filling the blank space with the request to let him become possessed with the same spirit, and see what happens." As I did this, his symptoms returned. His body began to rock, and he started talking in a language that did not make any sense. This went on for almost five minutes. I tried to understand the dynamics of healing, without any success. Once again, I used the mantra. This time, too, he returned to normal.

By this time, the audience became more interested in observing what I was doing than in watching the patient. A gentleman I knew quite well emerged from the crowd. He had a dominating personality. He threw his arm around me and said, "Rajmani, you are great! I never imagined that you had so much spiritual power. Can you show it again?"

I was already thinking to test my mantra again, and this fellow's admiration fueled my enthusiasm. Within a matter of minutes, the pilgrim was again possessed. This time, his symptoms were more violent. His body swung in the air, back and forth, left and right. He shouted louder. He even hit his head on the ground a couple of times. The crowd cheered, "Great, Rajmani, you are great!" Nobody cared how intense the pilgrim's pain was. People lifted me on their shoulders and danced joyfully. I became so drunk with self-recognition that I did not realize that the scene had turned into entertainment. One of the members of the crowd hugged me hard and said, "But, Rajmani, what do you do to control this spirit?"

By that time, I was totally out of my mind. "I'll show you," I said. I began to recite the mantra out loud with complete dramatization. I raised my hand as if I were a seasoned healer. I focused my gaze on the sufferer's face. And as soon as I finished reciting the mantra, he was healed. Once again, everybody shouted, "Bravo! Congratulations! Now I know where to go for help." Everybody left. I, too, went to bed, but due to excitement, I could not sleep at all.

In the morning, I took a ceremonial bath in the Ganga and rode my bicycle to Swami Sadananda's ashram. Unable to contain my excitement, I went to his room straight away. I paid my regards to him and said, "Swamiji, that mantra works. I am so grateful to you. It really works."

When I explained what had happened last night, he said in a sad voice, "I thought that you knew better than this. You ruined it. Remember, you had promised that you would not misuse it? That you would not show off? How childish of you. It was a *sabar* mantra. It works only if the secrecy is maintained. Now it's gone. Even if you teach someone, it will not work."

That day, I realized that mantras are living entities. They are not just words or phrases that you can learn from books. They are the focus of intangible yet potent spiritual powers that exert their effects on our body and mind, provided we know how to use them appropriately. Although I lost the power of that mantra, I was happy that I learned a big lesson: If you are lucky to have found a true master, then listen to him carefully. Do not show off.

Who Are These Gods and Goddesses?

Although I was embarrassed that I misused the healing mantra that Swami Sadananda had passed on to me,
the experience stirred up a series of questions in my mind:
Who are gods and goddesses? The healing mantra that
Swamiji had given me contained names of gods and goddesses from both Hindu and Islamic traditions. Was it
a Hindu or a Muslim mantra? There is only one God,
beyond name and form, number and gender. This
Supreme Being is the source of all powers. How is it possible for human beings to manipulate the power of the
Almighty? And yet that is what I seemed to be doing
when I used that healing mantra.

When I put my questions before Swamiji, he said,
"Human beings have a hard time going beyond the realm
of their minds. On one hand, they know the Supreme
Being is too big to fit in their small little heads, and yet
they wish it would fit. To reconcile fact with wish, they
project human characteristics onto God, and thus they
create gods in their own image. Then using the power of
faith, they breathe life into the gods they have created.
Thereafter they pray to these gods to help them overcome
their problems. These are lower-grade gods born from our
own minds. We empower them to help us overcome our
self-created misery. Once empowered, they become our
masters. And if we have confused minds, than we definitely
become their slaves and live at their mercy." To clarify this
subject further, he told me the following story:

Once there was a priest who earned his livelihood by
performing religious services for the people in his village.
He was a staunch devotee of Vishnu; thus people regarded

him as a holy man. Among his large following was a shepherd who wanted to see God—even though he had no idea what God was. His sheep didn't require much attention, so he had plenty of time to visit the priest and barrage him with questions about God.

The priest gave the shepherd all kinds of philosophical answers, but the man was so dense he could not grasp the intent of this discourse. Finally, in frustration, the priest thought of a way to explain God in a way that made sense to this simple man. He convinced the shepherd that God looks like a sheep—the healthiest and most beautiful sheep ever known. He instructed the shepherd to go into the forest and pray to this sheep God, and not to eat, drink, or sleep until God appeared. Delighted, the shepherd did exactly as the priest instructed.

On the third day, God came, but he looked like a beautiful human—except that he had four arms. He spoke, "I am very pleased with your devotion. Tell me, what boon do you wish from me?"

Startled, the shepherd asked, "Who are you? What are you doing here in the forest?"

"I am God," the beautiful man replied. "I came to fulfill your wish, because you have been praying to me."

"God looks like a sheep," the shepherd retorted. "You are fake. Get out of here. Don't waste my time."

The human-looking God left. An hour later, the sheep God came. He, too, said, "I am pleased with your devotion. Tell me, what boon do you wish from me?"

This time, the shepherd got up and greeted God, yet he wondered how a sheep could speak in human language and suspected he was being tricked again. So he said, "You look like God, but why are you speaking in human tongue?"

Immediately, God emitted a magnificent bleat. Then he said, "That is how I usually speak, but unless I speak your language, how can you understand?"

The shepherd was still skeptical, so he asked God to come with him so his priest could verify that he was really God.

"Wonderful," God replied. "Lead the way and I'll follow."

"You might change your mind," the shepherd replied. "Let me take you by the ear."

So it was that the shepherd arrived at the home of the priest, leading God by the ear. "Look, sir!" he called. "God is here!"

Annoyed, the priest came out and shouted at the shepherd, "It is a sheep, you idiot. You have lost your mind."

The shepherd began praying, "Oh God, help my priest to understand you."

The priest was also praying, "Oh Lord, help this foolish man to understand you."

As they prayed, God appeared simultaneously as Vishnu to the priest and as a sheep to the shepherd. At least, that's how they perceived it.

When the priest fell at the feet of the human-looking Vishnu, the shepherd thought he was prostrating to the sheep, so he, too, prostrated.

In order to bring the concept of God closer to our daily experience, we superimpose characteristics onto God that are compatible with our personal tastes, interests, preferences, and choices. In most religions, God seems to have only two main functions: reward those who worship him and punish those who don't. When you look at the world religions, you'll find that gods and goddesses have the same problems as humans do: their egos collide; they get into wars; they become infatuated with others' spouses; and they are punished by gods of a higher rank. Such gods are simply figments of our imagination, and yet, to faithful ones, they perform extraordinary feats. To non-believers, these gods fail to exert their powers. But once these gods and goddesses have seeped into the collective unconscious of a particular group of humanity, they exert their powers regardless of whether or not the members of that group believe in them at a conscious level.

A Healer Who Smelled like a Goat

Once I visited an amazing healer. Before he became famous and acquired a large following, he had been a medical doctor. But he smelled like a goat, and nobody wanted to be around him, including his family. He was virtually left alone. He had a very hard time making ends meet—his financial situation was so bad that he could not afford to get a haircut or have his clothes washed. At the pinnacle of his misery, however, the wheel of fortune suddenly turned. It happened when he began to look like a goat.

Despite his foul smell and his ugliness, he began drawing people's attention. With his big red eyes and long, wavy goatee, he could steal anyone's heart. Something also happened in the energy field that surrounded him, because wherever he walked, all the goats in the vicinity followed him. The news of this goat-energy spread like wildfire. People no longer cared about the aromatic discomfort that filled the air around him—he was a celebrity. Those known for their knowledge of Indian mythology and spirituality busied themselves digging into the mystery of this energy celebrity. They said that this great man must have done an intense meditation on the celestial goat which Agni, the fire god, uses as his vehicle. People came to believe he was a mystic whose connection to the celestial goat and the fire god gave him boundless healing power. Thus, the doctor who had lost his patients and his own family was now honored and visited by people from all walks of life seeking his blessing.

Like hundreds of other visitors, I went to see this healer. He lived in a three-story house, next to some small shops that sold flowers, garlands, cigarettes, and *paan* (slices of beetle nuts, tobacco, and other chewing ingredients, wrapped in beetle leaves). In any culture you don't visit a respectable person with an empty hand; you bring a gift with you. As soon as I arrived, several people told me that the most appropriate gift to offer to this healer was a packet of cigarettes, paan, and some money (not exceeding five rupees). So that's what I did.

To reach the healer, you had to pass through his waiting room on the first floor. The healer lived on the second floor, while the third floor was reserved for his special goats. By Indian standards, the second floor was quite magnificent. The living room, where he met his visitors, was large and well furnished. He sat on a cot and everyone else sat on the floor. Next to him was a container filled with herbal tablets that he himself had prepared. Visitors came in, placed their offerings at his feet, sat on the floor, and described their symptoms. The healer listened to their complaints lovingly and attentively and then took some pills from the container, blessed them, and gave them to the patients.

Like everyone else, I entered the room, bowed my head in respect, and placed my offerings before him. He looked at me, and to everyone's surprise, said, "He is the only one who has come to see me without seeking anything from me." Then he asked me to take my seat. He went on with his routine, asking about people's problems and handing over the blessed pills.

Finally, he turned his attention to me, saying, "I know curiosity brought you here, but tell me, what can I give you?"

I replied, "Your love."

"Once you have that from above, you get it from everywhere else. Now ask the question that you are holding back," he responded.

I asked him, "Doesn't anybody come with curiosity about what you did that enabled you to reach the state where you are?"

The mystic healer answered, "Not at all. Either people come seeking a cure for their disease or they come seeking faults and shortcomings in me."

"Will you please bless me by telling me something about yourself?" I urged.

"An unknown mystic taught me about the god Fire," he replied. "He instructed me to meditate on the personified form of the god Fire, sitting on his vehicle, the celestial goat. It was a tantric method of meditation. In part, I am happy with what I got; in part, I am not, because I do not know how to go beyond. The path I followed presented a miraculous result. I am blessed with a limited power to heal others, but the price I paid for that is evident. Look at me—I have to live with it. There is no way to go back."

Definitely, this healer was genuine. He was kind and generous. The herbal pills he gave with his blessings always showed miraculous results. He lived a comfortable life, but he did not exploit people's faith in him. What he shared with me about his personal life, however, aroused a curiosity greater than what I had before I visited him.

One day, when I was with my beloved teacher, Swami Sadananda, I told him of my experience with this healer. "Swamiji, he seems to be genuine," I said. "In his speech and actions, I found him kind and generous. I met dozens of people who were healed by him, but he told me he was not happy with himself. He also expressed that he wished he could attain freedom from what he had, but it seemed he had no choice but to live with it. Can you explain something about him?"

"He seems to be a *vama margi* tantric [a left-hand tantric]," Swami Sadananda replied. "His method of practice that enabled him to cultivate healing power must have included drug use."

"But, Swamiji, I thought left-hand tantrics employed

liquor, meat, fish, physical gestures, and sexual activity in their practice. The scriptures do not talk of drug use. Furthermore, there are strict requirements for undertaking left-hand tantric practices. How can drugs be used to cultivate healing power?"

"You are talking about a high-grade left-hand tantric," Swami Sadananda answered. "Such tantrics are rare. Their path is great and sublime. Before treading this path, they have mastered a high degree of self-discipline and self-understanding. But this healer you are talking about seems to be a tantric whose practice includes heavy use of drugs."

I argued, "But, Swamiji, he is kind and gentle. He is honest."

Swamiji replied, "He is kind and honest, that is why he is a good man. I know a little bit about him. He was an intelligent and diligent medical student who got involved in tantric practices without knowing much about tantra. As you know, lots of drug addicts today in India become sadhus. Many of them simply remain addicts, but some of them are transformed into drug-using mystics. Haven't you seen these sadhus—addicts and mystics—at the Kumbha Mela? His teacher must have been one of these mystics.

"The healer you met is kind and honest, but after all, he looks and smells like a goat. There must be periods when he thinks and behaves like a goat. In the normal course of life, it could be described as schizophrenia or another form of psychosis. From another standpoint, he is a mystic. From his own standpoint, he is a sick man. Because he is educated and honest, he knows that he has earned sickness from his practice. That is why he is looking for a cure. Because he is intelligent and kind, he is using an outcome of his sickness—his healing power—constructively to help others. That is why he is a saint."

Many good and sincere seekers end up doing shallow, and often unwholesome, practices. It is good to explore and venture into doing something new and exciting, but it is even more important to use common sense and to consult the authentic writings that address the nature and possible outcomes of such practices.

He Collects His Sheep
Before It's Dark

It was 1976. I was in the final year of my master's work. The health of my beloved spiritual preceptor, Swami Sadananda, was declining at an alarming rate. Since my first meeting with him, he had always inspired me to live a balanced life—to live in the world but remain connected to the Source.

I knew he was a great yogi, and I had always wanted to learn and systematically practice the full range of yoga, as he did. But despite the fact that he loved me very much, he listened to my requests to practice yoga under his supervision only partially.

During these moments he would say, "You don't need to become a yoga gymnast. Learn only what you need to learn, and make sure that you don't become a slave to what you have learned. Yoga is a spiritual path, and spirituality means not to linger anywhere. Practice and master the aspect of yoga that helps you keep moving. Practice such disciplines of yoga that enable you to come in touch with your inner self and allow you to understand the relationship between the individual self and the Supreme Being. Once you know your true nature, the charms and temptations of the world have no power to influence your mind. Through meditation, you start this inward journey; through meditation, you become established within yourself. The practices of yoga that prepare the mind for meditation are the only valid practices." So this great soul taught me yoga postures and breathing techniques selectively.

Although he himself was a renunciate, he taught his students how to live in the world and enjoy all worldly

Swami Sadananda

objects to the fullest. He owned nothing, but he inspired others to work hard and be successful in the world. Whenever I asked why he didn't teach the monasticism he himself practiced in his daily life, he would say, "In order to follow the path of renunciation and live a monastic life, you first have to have something to renounce. Renunciation is for those who are tired of having what they have and can no longer wait to find a more meaningful life."

Thus, for my intellectual stimulation, he inspired me to study and contemplate on the scriptures that advocated renunciation, but as part of my personal practice he insisted that I undertake spiritual disciplines that would enable me to become successful in the world. I knew he was an enlightened soul and would guide me in the right direction, and yet so many practices he taught were evidently not meant to give me freedom from the world, but rather, to bring me closer to the world.

Once or twice, when I asked him about this, he lovingly reminded me, "When you first met me, were you interested in wisdom or were you seeking divine protection? That morning, were you interested in knowledge or in living a peaceful, happy life? Remember, neither renunciation nor involvement in the world is your goal. Living a happy, healthy, and peaceful life, and gaining direct experience of your true self is your goal."

Now as he neared his last days, his attitude toward life somewhat changed. He no longer seemed interested in taking care of himself. He was coughing up huge amounts of mucus, but took medicines only when someone insisted. He was still actively helping others, but in relation to his personal life, he did not have any taste for it.

One evening, when I visited him, he was sitting outside on his wooden cot. The sun was about to set and he asked me to help him walk to his room. Once there, he seated himself on his wooden cot in his normal lotus pose and went into a coughing fit. I held him from the back and helped him while he discharged the mucus into an earthen bowl filled with lime powder. Not knowing how to express my feelings, I asked, "Swamiji, is there anything that can be done?"

He cleared his throat and said, "What can anyone do? Just like birth, death is a normal condition of the body." Then he asked me to bring some water from the Ganga.

I brought the water, and following his instructions, I left it in the water pot for a few minutes until the sediment settled. Then I gave him a glass of that water, and still sitting in the lotus pose, he drank it all. I found this unusual. For more than a year, he had been drinking only boiled, filtered water. I wondered why he drank water directly from the Ganga and especially so much at once.

In the dim light of the lantern, he began talking. After drinking the Ganga water, his symptoms of cough and cold disappeared. I found him as energetic as ever. He appeared to be in the mood of discussing spiritual matters. I knew that he was weak, so I felt uneasy making him talk, but he kept inquiring, "How are you? How is your practice? How are things at the university? Is there anything you desire of me?"

Not wanting to involve him in a prolonged conversation, I kept saying "fine" to every inquiry.

Finally, he said, "Ultimately, life culminates in death. Everyone sees it; everyone knows it. And yet, rarely does anyone prepare to face it, let alone greet it. Even the learned ones are afraid of death. This fear makes people become pitiful during the last moments of their life."

I knew that he was hinting at something. I realized that I must find the questions whose answers come only from the knowers of truth. So I asked, "Swamiji, how can one attain freedom from this fear and celebrate the concluding moments of life?"

He responded, "Birth means to emerge from the Divine Mother. To live means to play in her courtyard—nature. And death means to be reabsorbed in her womb. Once you know this, no fear will be left for you. Enlightenment means to know and experience that before birth, you were in her, and after birth, she is in you."

I said, "Knowing is easy, but it is the experiential part that is so hard."

"That comes from grace."

"That, too, I know, Swamiji," I whispered.

Swamiji said, "I understand what you are trying to say. Divine grace is not bound by any rule or law. It is unconditional. It is always there. Those fully blessed with divine grace are called blessed children of God. They are the divine shepherds. Their only job is to make sure that everyone returns home safe and sound before it gets dark."

I asked, "Then what is our role, Swamiji?"

He replied. "Your job is to continue walking with full faith that no matter what, He collects his sheep before it's dark. On the journey of life, when you really get exhausted, then simply stop and wait, and keep remembering that He will pick you up."

Then he signaled that I should leave. As a gesture of farewell, I bowed my head. As I was about to walk out, he asked me to close his door. Before doing so, I asked if he wanted me to leave the lantern. He replied, "What's the use of this lantern now?" I picked up the lamp. "Are you leaving?" he asked.

I replied, "Yes, Swamiji."

Then he spoke his last words, "The truth is, He is our master and all living beings are his sheep. Blessed are those who know this truth."

With reverence, once again I bowed my head, and with the lantern in my hand, I walked out.

That same night this great soul left his body. But his words, "He collects his sheep before it's dark," always resound quietly in my mind and grow louder when I begin to feel that I am lost.

CHAPTER FIVE

The Way
of Providence

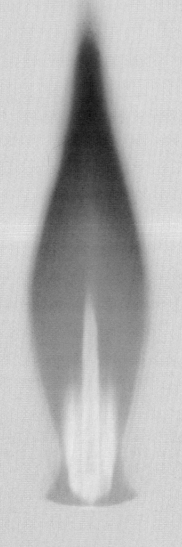

The Dream That Changed My Life

I had lost my teacher, Swami Sadananda, my spiritual guide who played a pivotal role in shaping my life for the past several years. I had spent my days at the university pursuing my academic goals, and the rest of the time I sat at his feet while he taught me the Vedas, the Upanishads, and many tantric and puranic texts. Under his guidance, I undertook spiritual practices that convinced me that God exists and manifests in numberless names and forms. The experiences I gained while being in his company had infused my heart with the conviction that one day I would have full realization of the Lord of Life. But now my teacher was gone, and caught between the demands of my worldly obligations and the inner calling of my soul, my conviction was put to the test.

I had just completed my master's degree and had entered the doctoral program in the Department of Sanskrit at the University of Allahabad. I had good grades and I was entitled to receive a scholarship from the University Grant Commission of India. Further, I had powerful connections that would help in securing the scholarship. But fear and anxiety gripped me so tightly that I kept running from Allahabad to Lucknow, and from Lucknow to Delhi, kissing the feet of professors, vice-chancellors, politicians, even clerks and secretaries in the office of the governor, hoping their favor would secure my scholarship.

When I got the scholarship, I regained my tranquility, at least momentarily. With that tranquil mind, I began to reflect: "Why was I suffering from anxiety? I did not have financial problems; in fact, for the last three years, I had been living a more comfortable life than many well-established people in India. I would have been just fine even without the scholarship. So what was my real problem? Is this problem over?"

As I contemplated, it became clear that I had been suffering from inner unrest ever since my spiritual teacher, Swami Sadananda, died. His last words, "He collects his sheep before it's dark," had left me torn between two worlds. From the core of its being, the soul within me had been crying, "God, God, God!"

Because for the past several months I had been preoccupied with my final exams, deciding what to do with my doctoral programs, and then getting this scholarship, I had not realized that deep within I was possessed by the inner calling of my soul. This realization threw me out of my ordinary realm of thinking and being. I found myself at a crossroads. Yet I was far from certain that any of these roads would lead me anywhere.

Worldly norms combined with family pressure were forcing me to find a job, but my inner calling demanded that I find something more fulfilling than simply trading time for money. After years of studying the scriptures and being in the company of Swami Sadananda, I knew the purpose of life was more than being born, growing into adulthood, struggling for worldly success, becoming old, and dying. I was convinced that it is better and more satisfying to shine for a flash than to smolder for years.

When my parents and sisters were not uppermost in my mind, I thought of leaving everything behind and exhausting all of my energy in walking toward the Lord of Life, who, as promised by Swamiji, "collects his sheep before it's dark." His words were always ringing in my head: "Your job is to continue walking. When you really get exhausted, then simply stop and wait, and keep remembering that He will pick you up." I often felt that I had not even started walking and I did not know what exhaustion meant. At this stage of my journey, what right did I have to stop and wait and fool myself, thinking He will pick me up?

As soon as I joined the Ph.D. program, a position opened for a lectureship at the university. I applied for it with a divided heart—half wanting it and half praying that I would not get it. My professor knew about my powerful connections and was confident I would get the job. What he did not know was how terribly I was caught in the war between wanting and not wanting this position.

Anand Pratap Singh, who was like my godfather, asked me more than once what I wanted and if I needed any help. Due to my inner conflict, which was destroying my peace of mind, I avoided everyone's help, including his. Seeking a resolution to this inner conflict, I resorted to my long-cherished tactic—surrender.

I prayed, "I am at a crossroads. To me, all the roads intersecting here are equally unfamiliar. All choices are equally doubtful." With this prayer, I resolved to undertake a special practice called *shata chandi* to propitiate the Divine Mother. It consists of one hundred recitations of a holy scripture called *Durga Saptashati*.

The night after I completed the practice, I had a dream. I was in a tall building, sitting on one of the steps of a stairway leading to the roof. Suddenly I found a five-year-old girl sitting in my lap. The upsurge of joy that I experienced from her presence told me that she was not an ordinary child. The beautiful aura on her face told me that she was the Wonder embodied. She was not of this world.

While all these thoughts were running through my dream, she asked, "Do you know the difference between good and pleasant?"

I said, "No."

She asked me again, "Do you know what is best and most auspicious for you?"

"No," I said.

Then she got up from my lap, stood in front of me, and lovingly slapped me on my cheek, saying, "Then why are you insisting on becoming a professor at the university?" With that, she ran up the stairs.

Still dreaming, I realized that she was none other than the Divine Mother. I also knew that she was exactly five years old, and thus, according to the scripture that I had just recited one hundred times, she was the mother of Ganesha and his older brother, Skanda. She was the Mother of Mercy! This understanding filled my heart with joy, and yet I felt sad because she had run up the stairs, leaving me alone on the lower steps.

I started chasing her. With her small legs, she ran faster than I could imagine. I ran and ran, and then totally exhausted, I sat down on one of the steps in despair. She leaned over the railing, and seeing my despair, the Mother of Mercy returned. She placed her hand on my head and said, "I know better than you about you. I am your life. Becoming a teacher at a university is not the highest thing in the world." With these words, she disappeared, and my dream was over.

I was happy that there would be no place for me in academic institutions, but still I went through the motions of competing for the lectureship. As providence had it, three days later, in a New Delhi hotel, I met a mysterious sage whose arrival in my life made up for the loss of my beloved teacher, Swami Sadananda. Thereafter, I was no longer in need of a job. The name of this mysterious sage was Swami Rama.

The Way of Providence

It was September of 1976. I had already started my doctoral work, but my mind was no longer on my studies. I simply went through the motions—visiting libraries, talking with my professors, and going for job interviews. Following the trail of interviews, one day I reached Delhi. It was my first visit. There I stayed with Anand Pratap Singh, who at the time was the personal assistant to Raja Dinesh Singh, the minister of external affairs in the government of India.

One morning, Anand Pratap Singh asked if I wanted to drive around New Delhi. I readily joined him. He drove for a while, showing me the important places, and then stopped his car in front of the Ashoka Hotel. He told me he had an important meeting there, and handing me a ten-rupee bill, said, "It might get late. Walk in this park and anywhere else that you wish, and then take a three-wheeler and go back home. No need to wait for me."

I took the ten-rupee bill from his hand and walked through the beautiful park until I reached its other side. Across the road there stood another magnificent hotel, the Akbar. Never before in my life had I seen such a big hotel. To me, in those days, "hotel" meant where you can go and eat—a restaurant—so driven by curiosity, I entered. The lobby was beautiful, but there was no food. I was a bit disappointed; but excited to see what might be in such a magnificent place, I decided to give myself a tour of the hotel. I took the elevator, got off on different floors, and walked around. From here, the park across the road through which I had just walked looked even more beautiful. I busied myself going from one floor to another, seeing the park from different heights. But as I stood at the window of the ninth-floor lobby, I was getting a little nervous. What would I say if someone asked what I was doing there? Who was I to be walking around this hotel? Just as I was thinking of taking the elevator and leaving the premise, I heard a sweet but loud voice say, "*Bete* [son]."

I looked toward the source of that voice and saw a tall, handsome man walking toward me dressed in a traditional Indian garb—silk kurta and pajamas. I knew that he was the one who had said "*Bete,*" and from the way he was looking at me, it appeared that he had been addressing me. I did not know this person and I wondered why he would call me. He walked up to me, put his hand on my head, and said, "When did you come?"

Somehow I felt he knew me very well and I knew him, too, but I was surprised that I was not able to remember who he was. He did not give me time to put any strain on my memory, but said, "What are you doing these days? Come. You have become so big." He took my hand in his, and without knowing why, I started walking with him toward his room. In response to his question, I told him that I had just completed my master's and I had started my research work. By this time, we reached his suite. Both of us sat on the couch. Then he asked, "What is the subject?" When I told him that my research was focused on tantra in general, and the exact topic was the philosophy of Sri Vidya, he laughed and said, "You'll get your Ph.D. and D.Litt. in no time, but tell me, when are you going to start your practice?"

I was bewildered. In his voice I sensed both a challenge and an invitation. Before this day, I had visited many great scholars, pandits, swamis, and yogis, but except for Swami Sadananda in Allahabad and Karpatriji in Banaras, I was not impressed with anyone. I had concluded that those who know do not readily teach, while those who do not know are dying to teach. Now, sitting in this hotel room, I felt in my heart this man was the one I had been waiting for, but my mind was asking, "Who is this man, so dominating and so overwhelming?" Suddenly I remembered Swami Sadananda's last words: "He collects his sheep before it's dark. On the journey of life, when you really get exhausted, then simply stop and wait, and keep remembering that He will pick you up." I wondered, "Is he the divine shepherd who has walked into my life to take me home safe and sound before it's dark?"

While these thoughts flashed in my mind at lightning speed, he spoke again, "I have also heard a little bit about this great esoteric science, Sri Vidya. What are the scriptures that talk about this science? Are they still extant?" His seemingly innocent and enthusiastic inquiry awakened the scholar within me and I began to converse with him comfortably. After thirty or forty minutes, my little store of knowledge was exhausted, and that is when he masterfully took over the conversation. As he spoke, I realized not only how profound was his knowledge, but also how deeply steeped it was in the unbroken lineage of the sages. Now I wanted to ask who he was but I felt it was too late to ask.

At the peak of our conversation the telephone rang. This man answered it and said, "Send him up." A few minutes later someone walked into his room. It was none other than Anand Pratap Singh, who a couple of hours ago had left me on the other side of the park in front of another hotel. Both of us looked at each other with disbelief, thinking, "How come you are here?"

This mysterious man asked Anand, "Why did you not bring this boy with you? I have been waiting for him."

"I wanted to, Swamiji, but without your permission, I hesitated to do it," Anand Pratap replied.

Soon after Anand Pratap Singh arrived, I realized that the mysterious soul I was talking to was Swami Rama, the sage who, according to my beloved teacher, Swami Sadananda, was the master of the esoteric science of Sri Vidya, as I have shared at length in *At the Eleventh Hour: The Biography of Swami Rama*. With this realization— I don't know how—my body swung around and I fell into his lap. I lost my awareness. I don't remember how long I stayed in that state. When I regained my normal awareness, all I remembered clearly is that Swamiji was wiping away my tears. I had a clear memory of an indescribable state of wonder and joy in which I had been absorbed. I tried to hold on to it.

Then I heard Swamiji saying, "I have been waiting for you. When are you coming to the States? You have to help me." He told me to get a pen and paper and he would write a synopsis of my thesis. I got up to get the items from the desk and I felt drunk. My mind was drawn to re-experience the joy it had tasted a few moments before, but by the time I brought the paper and pen, Swamiji had thrown a thick veil over my memory. Today the only thing I remember is that it superseded all the joys known in this world. Just the longing to re-experience that joy overshadows all the joys and sorrows of this world.

Months later, I asked Swamiji, "How did I come to that hotel? Did you know that I was coming? Was it a coincidence?"

Swamiji replied in two simple sentences: "The way of Providence is mysterious—nothing is accidental. Haven't you heard that a teacher appears when a student is prepared?"

Pandit Tigunait with his master, Swami Rama

Don't Be a Slowpoke

The day after our first meeting, I went to see Swamiji at his hotel. In contrast to the previous day, I found him wearing a Western two-piece suit. Today he did not look like a saint at all. With his black carry-on bag, he looked like a businessman ready to negotiate some deal. When, expressing my respect, I touched his feet, he exploded, "No need of this feet-touching business! Take this bag. We have to do some shopping." He handed his bag to me and walked out. I followed him.

At the portico, the driver stood with the car. Swamiji sat in the front next to the driver and pointed at the back seat, ordering, "Quickly take your seat!" I felt very odd because, according to Indian custom, the back seat is for those with status. I knew that the master had started training and taming his sheep. Finally the car stopped at Connaught Place, one of New Delhi's prominent shopping centers. Swamiji opened the door, got out of the car, and began walking toward the shops. I gently opened the door, looked around, made sure that nothing was left in the car, got out, and began walking toward him. By that time, he was at least fifty yards away and had stopped to wait. I ran, and as soon as I reached him, he exploded, "A slow person himself gets late and makes others late, too! Don't be a slowpoke if you wish to be with me." I got my first lesson.

According to the sages, if there is anything like sin, it is laziness. Procrastination and carelessness are the manifestations of laziness. If you are lazy, you will not start your work on time. If you don't start on time, you can never accomplish it. Success and laziness do not go together.

Twelve Nights in a New Delhi Park

Following his instructions, I visited Swamiji at his hotel early one morning. As soon as he saw me, he said, "Good, you are here. I am going to do some practice. Make sure nobody disturbs me. I'll be in my room. Under no circumstance come in unless I call you. If anybody inquires about me, simply say that I am not here."

With these remarks, he went in his room and did not come out until around two in the afternoon. He asked me to order some food for him from the hotel's kitchen, and once I did that, he told me to leave him alone: "You, too, have your lunch and come back quickly."

I took his commands literally. I went to a nearby restaurant, ate my lunch, and quickly returned to his suite. By that time, he had finished his meal. I picked up the dirty plates, put them out in the corridor, and closed the door while Swamiji vanished into his room. I passed my time in his living room. He emerged again at two in the morning. Just as in the afternoon, he asked me to order a meal for him, and once I did that, he dismissed me, asking me to come back before sunrise.

I knew that Swamiji did not want to be disturbed and I thought that if I went to Anand Pratap Singh's home, he might ask me about Swamiji. I would not be able to lie to him, but my honest answer might become instrumental in disturbing Swamiji. So I did not feel comfortable spending the night at Anand Pratap Singh's home. I could not stay at the same hotel, either—in the past couple of weeks, a number of the hotel staff had become familiar with me. I wondered where to go.

By the time I reached the main lobby, a thought flashed:

Shrine of Bhairav in Nehru Park in New Delhi

"It is so late. Why waste my time going anywhere? Nehru Park is just across the road. I'll spend the night there, and tomorrow, I'll think of a better place."

I went to the park and found it was closed. I climbed the high iron fence and dropped down into the grass on the other side. It was a chilly night. To keep myself warm, I walked around and exercised, and at sunrise, I returned to the hotel.

My routine for the next eleven days remained the same: sit on the couch in Swamiji's living room, order his lunch at two in the afternoon, run to a nearby restaurant to get my meal, guard him until two in the morning, order his meal, spend the night in the park, and go back to the hotel again at sunrise. On the twelfth night, when I was about to leave, Swamiji asked, "Where do you stay?"

"In New Delhi," I replied.

"Where in New Delhi?"

"Over there, across the road."

"Where? With someone?" he asked.

I said, "It's a wonderful place—very peaceful."

Then he asked firmly, "But where?"

"In Nehru Park, under the trees."

"But where do you eat?" he asked.

"In one of the *dhabas* [roadside restaurants]," I answered.

At this, his countenance changed, and putting his hand on my head, he said, "There will always be shelter for you. You will never go hungry."

Then, just as I had done the other nights, I ordered a meal for him. But this time, we ate together while he told me many stories of himself with his master. Finally, he asked, "Tell me, what can I give you?"

When I told him that all I wanted was his love and blessings, he said, "You already have that, but tell me, what can I give you? I promise that today I'll give you anything that you desire from me."

It seemed as if he were an ancient sage, not knowing what to do with his limitless wealth of love and compassion. He kept asking, "Tell me, what can I do for you? What do you want from me? Anything I have is yours. Take anything you want."

So finally I told him, "Swamiji, I want to see God."

"Do you want to see God or do you want to experience God?" he asked.

I said that I wanted to experience God, and he answered, "You will have it within a matter of a week or ten days."

It is this promise that took me to a coal-mining town in one of the eastern states in India, where even today, God, residing in thousands of shrines, awaits his devotees.

God at the Coal Mine

One day, when the predawn hours found me at Swamiji's feet, he said, "I will send you to see God tomorrow." I couldn't believe it. "It will be in the same region where once Mahatma Gandhi had the experience of God."

"Champaran!" I exclaimed.

"Not exactly in Champaran," Swamiji said, "but nearby. At a place called Giridih, near Jharia, in the state of Bihar."

I knew that Jharia was India's biggest coal-mining district, but I had never heard of Giridih. And without really thinking, I asked, "Swamiji, is there a shrine in Giridih? A cave or an ashram? Who is there?"

At this, Swamiji's eyes rolled inward, as though his soul had already reached Giridih. He spoke softly, "There are hundreds of shrines. Once you reach there, you will see them." Then after a short pause, he added, "Since you are going to be in the presence of God, no need of carrying too much baggage. Travel light."

Anyone who has ever traveled on an Indian train without a reserved seat will know that such a journey is in itself *tapas,* an austerity, a necessary purifying step on the way to finding God. This trip was no different. When the sun rose the next morning I pushed through a huge crowd and boarded the train, and after standing wedged between other passengers for a few hours, I finally managed to put my bedding on the floor and sit on it.

Remembering Swamiji saying that within a week or ten days I would see God, I was giving a spiritual interpretation to everything that happened around me. I felt God's grace when those next to me were in a friendly tone and when a macho fellow demanded that I squeeze myself into the corner so that he could commandeer most of my

A typical slum scene

bedding for his own seat. When I bought a cup of tea through the window at a station and the vendor walked away with the change, I was glad that God had arranged such an easy way for me to pay off my karmic debts. Screaming babies, the smell of unwashed bodies and human waste, the attempt to remember my mantra while people around me played cards, shouted, and fought—it all seemed like a glorious opportunity to maintain my inner equilibrium as I set out in search of God. And as the hours flew by and my destination drew nearer, anticipation was laced with joy. Two days after setting out, I disembarked at Dhanbad and caught a bus to Jharia, and then another to Giridih.

When I finally arrived at Giridih, rickshaw men rushed up offering to take me wherever I wanted to go. When I told them I didn't know exactly, one of them said, "Come, come. I know where everybody goes." I asked if there was a temple or a shrine or an ashram nearby, and he said, "Don't worry. I'll take you to the right place." He seemed honest but as time passed and we were still slowly winding our way through Giridih, I began to wonder if he thought I was a drug dealer, trying to fool him with my naive questions. Finally, after several hours, I spotted a run-down temple of the goddess Kali some distance from town and asked him to drop me there. By that time I'm sure he was convinced I was a seasoned dealer who knew exactly where to go to find customers. He accepted the fare I offered without the customary argument and drove away as fast as he could.

Next to the temple there were a few shops selling snacks, tea, tobacco, and paan, and behind that was a jumble of shabby dwellings where the coal miners and their families lived. It was obvious that this place was stricken by extreme poverty.

I was hungry and thirsty, so I went to one of the snack shops and ordered two *samosas* (potatoes wrapped in dough and deep-fried) and a cup of *chai* (spiced tea). The shopkeeper handed me the samosas on a plate made of leaves, but before I could take a bite, I noticed six pale children staring at the food. Beside them were two dogs so emaciated that their rib cages seemed about to burst through their skin. They wagged their tails weakly and then walked away, leaving the six children to gaze steadily at the food I was holding. I was extremely hungry but my body refused to accept a bite. So I split the samosas into seven portions, gave one to each of the children, and ate what was left. When I threw the leaves away, the dogs returned and listlessly licked at the remaining oil.

I had seen poverty before, but nothing like this. In holy places like Banaras, Allahabad, and Haridwar, visitors and pilgrims give a few pennies to the destitute because charity to the hungry in holy places ensures religious merit. But here there were no ashrams—and perhaps even no God. Here there was nothing but hunger and misery.

I was so overcome that I didn't know what to do or where to go. I had some money and could have gone back to town and stayed in comfortable lodgings, but I felt no inclination to do that. Instead I spent the rest of the day walking among the hovels, taking in the misery of the people who lived there. The thousands of men and boys who worked in the coal mines were so deeply indebted to the owners that when they returned after a long day's work they had barely enough money for a little flour or a handful of rice. Many of them sought oblivion in alcohol, which was cheap and readily available. Others turned to drugs. As evening drew near, smoke from hundreds of crude coal stoves engulfed the colony, and when night fell, fights broke out. In the dim lantern light I could see people crying, shouting, hitting each other. The tiny temple of the goddess Kali stood lifeless except at night when the drug addicts gathered there to gamble and fight.

Three days passed as I wandered among the colony's sagging bamboo huts with their tattered covering of soiled jute cloth and dirty plastic. In the evening and far into the night I sat beside a compost pile, which in the daylight hours was a grazing site for hens, roosters, and pigs. As I listened to the shouts and cries coming from the huts, I tried to figure out where God was. Is she in these slums? In these human hearts? Are these people suffering because of their karma? Or is poverty the result of ignorance? Does crime go hand in hand with hunger and starvation? Is there any truth to the scriptural statement that the poor and meek are blessed for one day they will see God? Who could be poorer than these people? Or more helpless and miserable? Do they have any sense of God? Lost in these reflections I did not realize how deeply my heart was sinking into an ocean of sorrow.

In the beginning some of the drug addicts sidled up to me, asking for some "stuff." I repeatedly said I had nothing, and eventually they left me alone. Others asked me what brought me to this place, and when I offered no explanation, they formed their own assumptions; many thought me insane. Then, late one afternoon as I was standing in front of the tea shop while the workers returned from the mine, I noticed a big car speeding toward us, leaving a trail of dust. The effect was electric: people scattered like chickens, shoving and pushing to get out of the way as a gleaming Mercedes flashed by without slowing, bathing the crowd in a thick cloud of dust. It was a *saheb*, one of the mine bosses.

Something in me snapped, and I could not stem the tide of fury coursing through my veins. "This is outrageous!" I exploded. "This man is exploiting you. You are less to him than the dust beneath his wheels!" My tirade had little effect on the crowd—people already thought I was a madman, so most of them ignored me. "How dare this man show off his luxury car here, under the eyes of these starving people?" I raged to myself. "He is sucking the very life out of them, stealing their labor and leaving them with only a few crumbs."

The incident had triggered the part of my unconscious where anger and violence were stored. Filled with rage and grief, I remained in the slum colony amid these suffering people. I was obsessed. I wanted to know more about them—how they live, why they fight and hurt each other, why they don't get up and walk away from this place. My dream of God-realization was abandoned.

Ten more days passed. I had not taken a bath or had a real meal. I slept under a tree next to the Kali temple, eating a bite here and there from the tea shop, trying to understand why Swamiji had sent me here. I knew he must have had a purpose, but instead of finding God, all I found was grief and anger.

Two weeks after I arrived in Giridih, I retraced my steps to Delhi. It was the same journey—one bus to Jharia, another to Dhanbad, and then two days on a packed train to Delhi—but this time the trip was very different. Everything in which I had recently taken such delight was now just another source of misery. The press of my fellow passengers in the crammed cars, the stench of sweat and excrement, the choking clouds of cigarette smoke, the screaming babies, the whining children, the shouting and joking and fighting only deepened my dark mood. The hours dragged. By the time I reached Delhi, it seemed as if I had been traveling for months.

When I met Swamiji again, the first thing he asked

was, "So, how was it? Did you see God?"

"All I saw was poverty," I replied, "and all I experienced was grief and anger."

"You went all the way to Giridih to come back with only grief and anger?" He paused, and after a moment he asked, "So what are you going to do with all that grief and anger?"

"I don't know, Swamiji," I replied.

With a serious look, Swamiji said, "Spirituality requires transformation—a qualitative change. When you can transform your grief into compassion and kindness, and when you can transform your anger into indomitable will and the power of determination, then you have begun walking on the spiritual path. When you see things inside or outside yourself, especially things you do not like, then try to understand their cause and their source."

"I have tried to do that," I replied. "It only made things worse."

"You have to compose yourself," he said. "When you are carried away by your emotions, you help neither yourself nor others. During such turmoil your mind is like a tiny fish caught in a turbulent stream: you can no longer think properly; your power of discrimination fails.

"Overall, you are a good boy. But when you saw the misery there in Giridih you lost your balance, and in that imbalanced state you were not able to remember the purpose of your visit. When you saw that rich man being driven by in a Mercedes, your anger exploded and you jumped to the conclusion that it was he who had caused all the misery you saw. And since then you have been hurting yourself with anger and violent thoughts. But your actions follow neither the voice of your heart nor the advice of your faculty of discrimination, and for this reason, even after seeing God, you couldn't see him. Even after being with God, you couldn't experience her."

"Where and how did I see God?" I gasped.

"It escaped you," he replied. "You were born in a learned family. You have studied the scriptures, and you are lucky to have received guidance from Swami Sadananda. And yet you could not overcome your habit of searching for God in temples and famous places.

"Priests say, and people believe, that in the presence of God all miseries vanish. But visit the holy places here in India or elsewhere in the world, and you will find that the holier the place is believed to be, the greater the misery surrounding it. That is where you find poverty, exploitation, violence, and hypocrisy. But love for God and hatred toward the children of God do not go together. That is why I sent you to Giridih. You needed this powerful jolt so that you could overcome your preconceived notions. There were hundreds of shrines in Giridih, but you walked among them without even knowing they were there.

"People build temples, churches, and mosques for God as though God is homeless and as if his home can be built by helpless people who depend on him. But in truth," Swamiji continued, "human beings are living temples of God. And how beautiful they are—a fully developed nervous system and brain, a mind equipped with the capacity for linear thinking, an intellect with the power of discrimination, and a soul blessed with the divine light that manifests in the form of free will and the power of determination. And in the innermost chamber of this temple, the Lord of Life resides.

"Searching for God and being with God means to come in touch with the core of your own being, where the Lord of Life shines in full glory. And in that light you begin to see yourself and the world around you in an entirely different way. This is called enlightenment. When you have achieved that, the world is not a prison, and to be in this world is not a punishment. Taking care of this shrine within you is called *puja* [worship]. Entering the inner chamber of this shrine systematically is called yoga *sadhana* [spiritual practice]. Not being caught by the charms and temptations of the world is called overcoming obstacles to spiritual practice. Being in the company of the Lord of Life within is called *samadhi* [spiritual absorption].

"The outer walls of this shrine—body, mind, and senses—are adorned with all forms of images. Some are erotic, others repellent; some are fierce, while others are gentle. Opening the door of your own heart is difficult. So if you wish to worship God, you had better take care of the temple.

"The gates of the big, wealthy temples are tightly locked—as are the hearts of the rich and powerful. Easier to open are the hearts of the poor. The shrines that are crumbling, the human hearts that are breaking, are where your worship of God will be most fulfilling. The Lord of Life dwelling in such hearts is waiting for those who can render their love and service, and serving these shrines will help you purify your own temple. You will become rich in heart and strong in mind."

Being in Swamiji's presence and hearing this discourse was soothing and inspiring, but deep down I knew I was still caught in my own emotional turmoil. "How can I begin my inner journey by serving the poor and opening my heart?" I cried. "First, I must gain emotional stability, mental clarity, and confidence in my own ability to hear and heed the voice of my soul. Worshipping God by serving the poor is a lofty goal, but how can I commit myself to nurturing others when I myself am so spiritually undernourished? I am confused and disoriented. And even though I know I have a master, a spiritual guide who loves me and is wise enough to show me the path, I am so caught up in my own turmoil that I have no motivation to do anything."

Swamiji smiled gently and said, "The Divine Mother is the source of true nurturance, my son. In her loving care you will find true protection. When my master was fed up with me, he threw me at her feet. She picked me up and held me to her bosom. You are fed up with yourself. That's a very good sign. Now, just as my master did to me, I'm going to throw you at her feet. And how she raises you and what she makes out of you is totally up to her." With that, he sent me to a shrine called Kamakhya in the state of Assam, east of Giridih. What happened there is another story.

Tantric Masters

The Shrine of the Goddess

Just a few days after I returned from Giridih, Swamiji told me to visit Assam, the easternmost state of India. As I was leaving, he said, "There visit the shrine of Kamakhya. This is where the Divine Mother will appear in the form of a guru and open the door to eternity."

I said, "But I have already found you."

"You don't understand," he replied. "Ritualistic practices are not part of our tradition. But you are being prepared as a teacher; you should know the path of rituals, too. It is in Kamakhya that the Divine Mother will make arrangements for you to practice that aspect of Sri Vidya. It involves rituals and the worship of Sri Chakra, and once you have learned that aspect of the practice, I will teach you the next."

From New Delhi, I took a train to Gauhati, the capital of Assam, and from there I took a taxi to the shrine of Kamakhya. It stands on top of a hill. Upon reaching there, I located the home of our ancestral priest. It had been more than seventy years since anyone from our village had visited this shrine, and the priest was thrilled to receive his traditional patron after such a long time. After a formal welcome, he pulled out his record book and showed me the name, address, and signature of a member of the royal family of Amar Garh to prove that I had reached the right place—we were not strangers. Then he gave me a brief introduction to this shrine: "It is the shrine of the Divine Mother," he told me. "Here, she is known as Kamakhya, the wish-fulfilling mother. Those who visit her never go away empty-handed. The best way to worship and propitiate her is to worship a virgin woman. Unless you have a respectful attitude toward women, you will not be able to receive her grace here. The tradition of virgin worship is unique to this shrine. Those who do not adore womankind cannot reach her."

I asked him, "How do you perform virgin worship?"

He answered, "If you wish to do this highest of all practices, I will arrange it for you. In fact, the door leading to the cave where the Divine Mother resides opens only after virgin worship."

The priest made all the arrangements. He bought a set of clothes, jewelry, cosmetics, and ritual objects that are specific to this particular worship. His own nine-year-old daughter was the virgin mother. He took me to the temple hall. There, two more priests came to assist him in the worship. I took a bath, put on clean clothes, and, as guided by the priests, completed the purificatory practices as a prerequisite to this worship. The virgin worship lasted almost two hours. It was an overwhelming experience.

Then the priest took me to the shrine of the goddess Kamakhya, located in an underground cave. The passage leading to the shrine was narrow and dark, but holding an oil lamp in my hand, I squeezed through the passage and finally reached the shrine, a natural rock that resembled the female organ. From this sacred triangular rock flowed a perennial stream that disappeared into the ground just a few feet away. On one side of this rock there was room for a few people to sit. The priest instructed me to place the lamp on the floor, and then he asked me to join him in

The main temple of Kamakhya

reciting the prayer in praise of the Mother. When the prayer was over, he said, "Now close your eyes and listen to the music of silence."

I sat there, quietly. Within a matter of a few moments, I felt as if my self-awareness was dissolving into the space that filled the cave. I knew that I was there; I could easily see my body, and yet I could not feel my existence. I heard the priest saying, "Now you can dip your hand in this perennial stream and repeat your mantra 108 times. Here, the repetition of mantra bears fruit a millionfold."

I put my hand in the water, but to my surprise, I forgot the mantra that I had been repeating since childhood. Holding my hand in the water, I tried my best to recollect the mantra, but I went totally blank. I feared that soon the priest would ask me to get out of the cave and I would miss this opportunity forever. In a panic, I started praying to the shrine, "Please help me remember at least one mantra." At first it seemed as if my prayer wasn't working. Then suddenly, a verse from the renowned scripture the *Bhagavad Gita* began to ring in my head: "Today I find myself at a total loss. I am overcome by anxiety. I do not know what is the right thing for me. What should I do? You are my master; I am your student. Please guide me on the path that is most auspicious and good. I surrender myself to you."

I took this verse as a mantra. I repeated it ten times while keeping my hand immersed in the water. A boundless peace descended upon me. My mind, blank just a second ago, was now filled with gratitude for the Mother whose energy filled this cave. As I was about to come out of the cave, the concluding words of prayer pulsated on their own in my heart: "Homage to the Mother of Mercy, who quiets our minds, and in the light of her love, reveals herself."

In a space charged with peaceful energy, as this one was, the mind automatically becomes calm and tranquil. The first and foremost sign of divine grace is that we acquire a peaceful mind. One who guides us on the path of peace is a teacher. A place that quiets our mind, lightens our heart, and uplifts our soul is a shrine. A place that opens the door to a peaceful mind is the house of God.

Dancing on a Sword

The shrine of Kamakhya is known for its miraculous powers. The entire hill where it is located is known as "Magic Hill." Since childhood, I had been hearing fantastic stories about this shrine and the region surrounding it. Even today, in villages throughout India, people believe that everyone in the state of Assam, particularly those who live in Kamakhya, know magic. In north Indian villages, mothers are terrified at the prospect of their unmarried sons going to Assam, for they believe that Assamese women have the power to turn them into goats during the day and exploit them at night by turning them back into men. I did not have any interest in gaining such experience, but I was curious as to whether there was any truth to these stories.

My first impression of Kamakhya was that it was a beautiful and peaceful place. Unlike other holy places in India, the priests of Kamakhya were gentle, loving, and kind. In other places, the less you interact with the custodians of the holy sites, the smaller the holes in your pocket and the greater your peace of mind. To me, the fact that the priests in Kamakhya were content with what they had, and there was not the slightest trace of greed and manipulation in their speech and actions, was magic in itself. This is why I decided to live at the home of my family priest next to the shrine. I stayed with this family for three months.

Late one morning, as I was about to finish my meditation and scripture recitation, one of my host's grandsons ran into my room shouting, "Come, come—quick! Mother is dancing!"

The boy was so excited he was not able to complete his sentences. He ran frantically from one room to another room, trying to get every member of the family to come out and watch some kind of unusual dance. Half of my mind was reciting the scripture and the other half was attending to what this boy was trying to tell us. Finally my host came in and reported, "Divine Mother is dancing on a sword. It is a rare phenomenon. It happens only once or twice in decades. You don't want to miss it."

Pointing to my lips, I hinted that I was in the middle of scripture recitation and I could not speak or get up from my seat. The priest demanded, "Just sip the sanctified water, stop the recitation, come and take a glance at this celestial dance, receive her blessings, and then resume your practice."

Although I did not know what was going on, I was sure it was something very special. Once outside, I heard the ceremonial drums, louder and more rhythmic than I had ever heard them before. All the men and women, young and old, were rushing to the southern grounds of the main temple, where ceremonial animal sacrifices are performed. My curiosity had brought me to this spot many times before. Each time, when I saw an animal being sacrificed, I wondered, "What is this cruelty? How could the Mother of Mercy devour her own children? She is said to be most benign and beautiful, but what could be more ugly and disgusting than drinking the blood of a helpless animal? This sacrifice business has nothing to do with worshipping a goddess; it is barbaric, and is simply an act of the beast within us."

When the priest and I arrived, thirty to forty people were standing before the sacrificial altar. I pushed through the crowd, and there, to my surprise, I saw a young man dancing barefoot on the sharp edge of a sword smeared with blood. At first, I thought that it was the blood from the dancer's feet; then I realized it was the blood of the buffalo that had just been sacrificed. The body of that buffalo was still lying on the ground behind the sacrificial altar.

The sacrificial altar behind the main temple of Kamakhya

I had seen many vigorous dances before, but never one like this. As the beat of the drum accelerated, the dancer's energy began to burst from his every pore. Soon my eyes could not assimilate all of his movements. He no longer seemed human. The vibrant energy emitting from his body pushed the crowd back several feet. The drums became louder and faster. The audience cried joyfully, "Hail to the Divine Mother! Hail to the Divine Mother!" Finally, the man collapsed and fell to the ground with a thud. Now the priests began to recite their prayers, and elderly women rushed to the dancer's aid with their palm-leaf fans. Ten minutes later, he regained consciousness and walked away with no memory of his dance.

Later, my host explained, "Once in a while, the Divine Mother descends from her heavenly plane and enters the body of her chosen child. It happens only once every few years. This phenomenon is totally unpredictable. The person infused with the divine energy loses his sense of self-identity. He walks freely and talks freely. His every word is revealed for it flows from a higher source. Her blessings bear instant fruit. After performing her celestial dance, she ascends and is reabsorbed into her transcendental essence."

Just as with many other mysteries, the question of whether animal sacrifice is a primitive custom grounded in superstition or a valid spiritual practice may be resolved as we climb the next ladder of our evolution. But the dance on the sword heightened my conviction that a human being is endowed with infinite potentials. To a large extent, these potentials are in their dormant state, but through our sincere effort and God's grace, they can be awakened. Spiritual practices that are meant to purify the way of the soul eliminate obstacles to our spiritual growth, but sometimes divine grace takes its own course, and as it descends, all impurities are washed off. When that happens, those who are so blessed experience their oneness with the Divine. Their connection with the Divine enables them to become perfect conduits for the energy that supersedes the rules and laws of our known world. In every culture we hear of extraordinary phenomena surrounding such people. When we see these phenomena through our own eyes but don't know how they happen, we call them miracles. But when we know how, we attribute such happenings to the limitless powers of God.

The Drummer Saint

During my stay at Kamakhya, I wanted to study with a living master. Even today, Kamakhya is the stronghold of tantric practices, especially the practices belonging to left-hand tantra. This particular path of tantra is ritualistic and employs alcohol, meat, fish, physical gestures, and even sex in its practices. Some tantrics also take drugs as part of their ritual practices, so it was hard to know who was really a mystic and who was simply a drunk. I knew there were adepts near and around the shrine, but I did not know how to recognize them. So I put my problem before my host and asked him to help me find a genuine master of tantra. He suggested several names, and the one who stood highest on the list was Damaru Baba. His real name was Charanand Nath, but people called him Damaru Baba because wherever he went, he always carried his *damaru*, Shiva's drum.

Damaru Baba was an amazing saint. He lived just a few hundred yards below the main shrine in the valley of the Brahmaputra River, in a small hut surrounded by cobras and deadly poisonous iguanas. Everyone knew him and everyone respected him, but rarely did anyone have the courage to visit him. My host spoke very highly of him, but advised me not to visit him. I insisted, so he finally told me precisely how to reach the place where this saint lived and gave me permission to visit this master in the afternoon—provided that I return before sunset.

When I reached there, I found Damaru Baba sleeping in his hut. I sat quietly outside his door under a tree for an hour or so, meditating on my mantra and trying to banish scary thoughts about the snakes and iguanas and lepers, who according to the local people, shared the same terrain. Then I heard the saint clearing his throat and chanting hymns from the Vedas. I came closer to the hut, waiting for the right moment to knock at his door. As I approached, a voice came from inside, "Come in, but be careful." Then I heard him talking, "You go to the other side. No, no, no— that side. And be quiet." I opened the door and there I saw his friends, the cobras. Damaru Baba said, "Please sit down. Don't be afraid of them. They are my friends; they protect me from intruders."

I paid my respects and sat on the floor, but I was terri- fied. Two cobras were coiled and staring at me. I wondered how many more there were. The saint knew that my heart was refusing to beat inside my rib cage. Feeling pity for me, he asked his friends to leave for a while. Five cobras slith- ered out of his hut, followed by three iguanas. Then the saint said, "All of them are gone. Please be comfortable." He offered me some roasted potatoes and water.

After the formal hospitality was over, he asked me where I was from and how long I had been here. When I told him that I had been here for almost a week, he was surprised: "Why have you been here for that long? A day or two are enough to see everything here. What are you searching for?"

I replied, "I'm from Allahabad. I am doing my Ph.D. on Sri Vidya, which is at the core of tantric philosophy and practice. I feel that writing a dissertation on this subject without some direct experience would be misleading; therefore I wish to learn from a living master and practice under his supervision."

He laughed and said, "Unless you already have one, you could not have reached here. Tell me, who is your teacher? If he knew about this place, then he must have been here. If he has been here, he must have practiced the science that you want to learn and practice. And if he has practiced it, then why wouldn't he teach you himself?"

The entrance to the shrine of Koti Linga in Kamakhya

I told him the brief story about my father, my training in Sanskrit, my first teacher, Swami Sadananda, and finally, of Swami Rama. He closed his eyes for a few minutes, and then spoke softly, "You deserve someone better than me." I could not believe what I heard, for during the brief time he had sat with his eyes closed, I experienced the same peace I felt when I first met my master, Swami Rama. In my heart I felt that this saint was a great adept. This statement, "You deserve someone better than me," was either a reflection of his humility or he was trying to get rid of an unworthy student.

With all humility and honesty I protested, "Baba, why do you say that? Where in the world can I find a master like you who lives in perfect harmony with Nature and all her children? Please do not toss me out. If I am not prepared, then guide me so that I may prepare myself to study with you."

"No, no—please do not misunderstand me," he responded. "I can teach you and I will teach you. But I will not advise you to follow my path. My path is extreme. As a young man, on the spur of the moment, I left the world. In my ignorance, I was looking for a quick fix for my spiritual hunger. And for that, I was ready to pay any price.

"As you know, here in Kamakhya, people practice the aspect of tantra that incorporates liquor and drugs. I used heavy doses of marijuana to kill my sense cravings so I could do my practices without any distraction. I accomplished that goal, but only at the cost of turning into a marijuana addict. So I am here by myself. I live with the children of Mother Nature. They love me and I love them, but I am useless to human beings. All I can share with them is what not to do in life. You are educated, and blessed with a teacher who has a broad understanding of life in general and spirituality in particular. That is why I said that you deserve someone better than me."

I begged, "Baba, regardless of whether or not you teach me through words, please give me your blessings. If you introduce me to an adept, I will consider it the highest form of blessing."

The saint guided me to another adept, Dolai Baba, who, according to the learned people in the region, was the blessed son of the Divine Mother. That is how, a few days later, I met my tantric master, who taught me the aspect of tantra that involves rituals.

Honesty is the highest of all virtues. How great, therefore, are the masters who tell the truth even if it means exposing their own weaknesses. Thus, they guide seekers on the path with the fewest bumps and pitfalls.

The tantric master Dolai Baba (Pramath Nath Avadhut)

My Tantric Master

My host at Kamakhya took me to the renowned tantric master, Dolai Baba, late one afternoon. He was just getting ready for his evening walk. Upon seeing me, he asked my host who I was. When he told this saint about me, Dolai Baba said, "Why did you bring him here? He is your client. A priest bringing his client to another priest doesn't make any sense." My host told him that he brought me to him at the request of Damaru Baba, the drummer saint. At this, Dolai Baba laughed and said, "That drummer, the friend of beasts, is lost in his own world. He tricks others into getting lost in the same world. He can't use me in his trickery." Then signaling to me that he did not want to be bothered, he left for his walk.

I reported the outcome of my meeting with Dolai Baba to the drummer saint. He told me not to give up—that I should visit him every afternoon until he accepted me. When I visited Dolai Baba the next day, the first thing he said was, "I am a priest. All I do is perform rituals and pray for Her mercy. You are a learned scholar from Allahabad. Why do you wish to waste your time learning rituals from a priest?"

I replied, "Baba, I am not interested in priestly rituals. I want to learn the ritualistic science of tantra that, in modern days, is shrouded in mystery. I have read a few scriptures, but what I gleaned from them is incomplete and fragmented. I need someone like you to show me the missing links. Please do not reject me. Your friend the drummer, who is lost in his own world, has thrown me into the soil that is you. The soil doesn't reject the seed, for it is against the law of nature."

Under a most mysterious circumstance, four days after this conversation, Dolai Baba accepted me as his student, and I began to spend most of my time with him.

As time passed, I realized that Dolai Baba was one of the most learned persons in the region, not only in terms of his experiential knowledge but also in academic matters. He had completed his higher studies in Banaras and returned to his home at Kamakhya as an acclaimed scholar of Sanskrit and scriptures. Thereafter, he dedicated his life to the study and practice of tantra. The spiritual path he personally followed is known as *kaula* tantra.

The word *kaula* is derived from *kula*, which means "family." As the name itself suggests, kaula is the path of spirituality that can be practiced while living in a family. It is a path of freedom in the world, rather than freedom from the world. The practices belonging to this tradition are supported by the philosophy that proclaims that everyone and everything in this world is a member of one family. Transcendental primordial energy known as the Divine Mother is the head of the family and the origin of all that exists. All forms of matter and energy emerge from her. It is not that the universe as a distant entity evolves from her; rather, she herself manifests in the form of the universe. She *is* the universe. Experiencing ourselves to be different from her is ignorance, and it is this ignorance that leads to bondage. The sense of separation from her results in strife. Experiencing our oneness with her is self-understanding and leads to liberation. It is the experience of unitary consciousness that brings all forms of strife to an end.

From the moment of our birth, we have been identifying ourselves with the physical realm, especially with our bodies. This identification confines our consciousness to the pleasure and pain and loss and gain associated with our physical level of existence. So often we find ourselves driven by the four primitive urges: food, sleep, sex, and self-preservation. Upon analysis, we find that all emotions, such as desire, anger, hatred, jealousy, and greed, spring from these four primitive urges. Unless we rise above our body consciousness and become established in non-dual unitary consciousness, these emotions will continue to flood our minds and nervous systems with anxiety, fear, and a pervasive sense of insecurity. If, on the other hand, we follow the path of self-discipline and inner purification, we eventually attain freedom from these urges and the emotions springing from them.

I stayed with Dolai Baba for almost three months. He taught me the esoteric aspect of tantric rituals and showed me how to sanctify ritual objects, how to draw yantras and mandalas, and exactly how to meditate on them. Most fascinating among all the rituals was the one pertaining to sanctifying alcohol and removing its deluding effects on the mind.

The Art of Joyful Living

After leaving Dolai Baba, I returned to Swamiji in New Delhi. In the days that followed, I kept remembering that even though Dolai Baba had taught me tantra, he had repeatedly stressed the importance of practicing yoga as well. I clearly remembered him saying that without the practice of yoga, a student of tantra may become imbalanced, even delusional.

During our evening walks in Kamakhya, he had pointed out several tantrics who apparently possessed a remarkable level of supernatural powers and yet were lopsided in their daily lives. Many of them used drugs to stay "grounded." Some suffered from insomnia, because as soon as they closed their eyes, their minds became crowded with visions pertaining to extraterrestrial realms. Others suffered from unwanted fits of "spiritual bliss" that frequently gushed forth, as they claimed, from their union with the deity they worshipped, causing their nervous systems to shake as if they were having an epileptic seizure. Citing those tantrics, Dolai Baba would say, "See, this is what happens when people follow an extreme path without being fully grounded in the practice of yoga." But whenever I asked him what he meant by yoga, he would simply reply, "Here, yoga means raja yoga as taught by the great sage Patanjali."

At the earliest opportunity, I briefed my master, Swamiji, about my experiences while living at Kamakhya. I also told him that while teaching tantra, Dolai Baba constantly admired yoga.

"Can you explain," I asked Swamiji, "what exactly is yoga? To me, at the physical level, yoga means practicing asanas; at the mental level, it means gaining control over the modifications of the mind. What kind of yoga helps us prepare the foundation for undertaking other forms of practice?"

That day, Swamiji was in a great mood. In fact, it seemed that he was waiting for this kind of question. What follows is an almost verbatim account of how he explained yoga to me that day:

"Yoga means union, for it helps you re-establish a harmonious balance among different aspects of your being—body, mind, consciousness, the world within you, and the world outside you. It can help you explore unlimited potentials within yourself and ultimately find meaning and purpose in life here and now.

"After hundreds of years of constant practice, self-observation, contemplation, and self-analysis, the great masters in the East concluded that to be born as a human is in itself the greatest achievement and to die without knowing the purpose of life is the greatest loss. The system of philosophy and practice that can help you find meaning and purpose of life, and not let life go in vain, is called yoga.

"Yoga consists of a set of techniques that can enable you to gain access to the limitless wealth that lies dormant in your body and mind. It also helps you understand who you are, what you are made of, why you are here, and where you will go after you die. The great sage Patanjali, who gave final shape to the philosophy and practice of yoga, tells us that you have a body, but you are not the body; you have a mind, but you are not the mind. Both body and mind are given to you so that you can complete the journey of life, reach your destination, and recognize your blissful self. Yoga offers tools and means for making the best use of body, mind, and senses, and achieving that which the soul could not have achieved without interacting with this beautiful creation.

"Nowhere else than in yoga can you find such a simple, straightforward, and effective way of interacting with the world, becoming a healthy and happy person, and enjoying the objects of the world without getting lost in them. Yoga offers you the tools and means to have a successful and productive life without becoming a slave to your own success and productivity. Yoga is a way of self-mastery, for by practicing yoga, you become master of yourself—master of the world within and the world outside you.

"I went to the West," Swamiji continued, "with great expectations. I thought people in the West had scientific minds; that they were sincere, hardworking, and believed in self-effort. My expectations shattered in the 1970s when I traveled the width and breadth of the United States and noticed that people in this country followed cults, dogmas, and superstitions as much as people everywhere else.

"I did scientific experiments on yogic practices, breathing exercises, concentration, and meditative techniques at the Menninger Foundation in Topeka, Kansas. I made sure that people understood that yoga wasn't magic or a religious cult, but it was hard to convince people, especially those who expected a swami, guru, pandit, or a priest to take care of all of their problems. I realized that, to some, yoga was just a part of physical fitness, and to others, it was an esoteric path. I met only a few students who understood that yoga is a path of physical well-being and mysticism and something beyond. I was surprised at how many false and incomplete teachings were introduced in the name of yoga and how commercialism had contaminated this sublime science.

"Yoga in its own right is a systematic science. Its practices are supported by a profound philosophy known as Samkhya. Yogic techniques are scientific in the sense that you can clearly see a causal relationship between the practices you undertake and the results you achieve. Through their repeated experiments, yogis have mapped out all possible mistakes that you may commit during your practice; therefore they warn you beforehand about what you must not do in the practice of yoga.

"The yogis have made this science even more complete by combining the principles of ayurveda and the time-tested techniques of rejuvenation known in the East as *rasayana*. And today, by using the principles of holistic health, diet and nutrition, and modern psychology, you can derive even greater benefits from the practice of yoga. But if you are not familiar with the philosophy on which yoga practices stand, then you may fail to see yoga's vast scope. Consequently, you may end up practicing just a few yogic techniques here and there and achieve very little benefit.

"In the practice of yoga it is very important to know that yoga is not a religion, although yogic principles are an integral part of most religions. Most religions of the world normally teach what to do, but they do not teach how to do it. They also teach what not to do, but do not teach how to avoid doing it. Yoga, on the other hand, teaches not only what to do, but how to do it. But if for some reason you can't do it, it is not a sin; simply try again. Unlike most religious paths, in yoga there is no room for guilt and self-condemnation. Yoga teaches you to acknowledge the fact that you are a human being and as such you have certain strengths and weaknesses. Try your best to overcome your weaknesses.

"Due to the intelligence and free will that you have received from Providence, you have the freedom to cultivate higher virtues and overcome negative traits. And yet, you may have certain weaknesses that prevent you from accomplishing everything you wish and plan. In that case, learn the art of performing your actions skillfully.

"When you meet with success, do not let your inner equilibrium be overcome by excitement. When you meet with failure, do not let yourself sink into depression and sadness. Gaining and maintaining this equilibrium is called the art of joyful living and is the foundation for self-mastery. This art of joyful living is at the core of yoga."

CHAPTER SEVEN

Touched *by* Fire

My Personal Bible

A few days after I returned from Kamakhya, Swamiji said that it was now time for me to do his work in the West. "But you have a problem," he said. "You still think like an Indian. You behave like an Indian. You measure others' values with your Indian yardstick. My work is not confined to India or any particular culture, but the center of my mission is in the United States. You have to work with the people of America and you have to live with them. Before you work and live with them, you have to know who they are. You have to know their cultural, social, and philosophical background."

I asked, "Swamiji, should I study some books on American history and culture?"

"It will take ages to get a good understanding of the culture by reading books," Swamiji replied. "I will give you a crash course. America is the land of limitless opportunities. Those seeking religious and economic freedom founded the nation. Through their hard work, they have gained these freedoms to a great extent. For the past two hundred years, the United States has been continually growing stronger. Now it has become a superpower, but at a subtle level, the majority of its citizens have become victims of their material prosperity. They do not know how to use their worldly success to find long-lasting peace and happiness. Let me tell you why.

"After World War II ended in 1945, the United States was blessed with a booming economy. Economic opportunities drew people away from their hometowns and their extended families. This mobility granted them greater freedom at a personal level, but took away the emotional support and guidance that naturally flows from an extended family. After World War II, people made more money in less time and had more leisure. Television and other forms of mass media flowed in to fill it. As you know, the more you have, the more you want. The growing prosperity in the external world fueled an insatiable desire for more and more worldly objects. The entire culture became materialistic and outward-oriented. The more they searched for pleasure and comfort in the external world, the more they began to lose touch with their inner selves. The growing prosperity in the external world, coupled with a growing sense of emptiness in the inner world, gave rise to the culture of the sixties and experiments with alternative lifestyles, religious beliefs, and spiritual practices.

"It was during this period that my master sent me to the United States to create a bridge between East and West and between spirituality and science. As I traveled and lectured the length and breadth of the country, I made a careful study of the cultural psychology of American society. I found that family ties had been loosened, old values were falling away, and new values had not yet been formed. Even though the economy had engendered an insatiable desire for an endless number of objects, deep down, people were questioning the purpose and meaning in life.

"When I came to the United States, the culture of the sixties had reached its climax. Recreational drug use and casual sex had become the norm among many groups of young people. Demand for fulfillment in the inner world and outer world had attracted people from all over the world, but especially from India, Tibet, China, and Japan. The general impression Americans got from this influx was that anything out of the ordinary was spiritual: kung fu, karate, tai chi, reiki, dream therapy, mind reading, clairvoyance, astrology, crystal healing, tarot cards, hatha yoga, different forms of meditation—all were lumped together in the broad category of spirituality. The most alluring spiritual teachers were those who promised miraculous experiences such as *shakti pata* [the direct transmission of spiritual energy], out-of-body experiences, astral travel, visions of gods and goddesses, and other forms of psychic experiences, including those engendered by psychedelic drugs.

"Following the instructions of my master, I brought the knowledge of the Vedas and Upanishads to the West. I presented the teachings of the Vedic sages through yoga. My style of teaching attracted those who were interested in self-transformation, but many came to me only after they realized how much harm they had already done to themselves by living carelessly. So I founded the Himalayan Institute, and using it as a platform, I began to teach the philosophy of life: Human life is the greatest gift from Providence; a human being is endowed with infinite potentials; you can unfold your potentials by practicing techniques of yoga. I do not encourage people to run away from the world; rather, to recognize what is great, glorious, and useful in themselves, to unfold and embrace that which helps them find meaning and purpose in life, and to discard that which serves as obstacles in their overall growth. I teach people how to attain freedom from inner slavery. I repeatedly remind them that the mind is the greatest of all mysteries. Knowing yourself means knowing

Pandit Tigunait's master, Swami Rama

your mind. My message is the message of the sages: Study the dynamics of the mind; refine it; train it; and by using it properly, you'll be able to see that this world is a beautiful place and you are a beautiful being.

"I have been in the United States for almost ten years," Swamiji continued. "But because I am a swami and I come from India, a great number of people identify me as a religious teacher. I remind them again and again that I am simply a servant in a long lineage of the sages, and that the sages do not belong to particular religious or ethnic groups. But people have a hard time understanding this. I have been reminding them constantly that simply changing religions and adopting a new lifestyle will not lead them anywhere. It is self-transformation that will bring true fulfillment in life.

"My master has given me a very difficult task. When you come to the States, you will know what it takes to be a teacher. To be appointed as a teacher is also a great privilege. If you are honest and if you are vigilant in delivering only what you have received from the lineage and that which you have verified through your personal experience, then you will experience a great sense of joy in every moment of your life. The important thing is that you first put yourself in the shoes of those whom you are supposed to serve. Then you will automatically know what to teach and how to teach."

This brief description of American culture and Swamiji's approach to health and spirituality has helped me understand how to deliver the ancient wisdom to modern people. Today, Western culture dominates the world, and the need for recapturing peace of mind is growing exponentially. Swamiji's approach to spiritual development and total well-being is as appropriate and vibrant today as it was

thirty years ago. His brief description of materialistic culture is, to me, like the book of Genesis in the Old
Testament. His approach to cultivating a quiet mind and
reconnecting ourselves with the core of our being is the
master remedy that cures all diseases.

A Test of Patience

It was October of 1979 when I first came to the United States. After spending three days at the Himalayan Institute's headquarters in Pennsylvania, I went to Minneapolis. There I stayed at the Meditation Center. The center's founder, Dr. Arya, and his wife, Lalita Arya, embraced me as part of their family. In those days, Swamiji's two very blessed students, Rolf and Mary Gail Sovik, lived at the center. For all practical purposes, they were my guardians. The love I received from them is a treasure that continues to compound to this day.

As usual, Swamiji had gone back to India for the winter. From there, he called people throughout the States, especially in Minneapolis, making sure that they told me how happy he was with me. They relayed his comments to me: "Panditji is a brilliant man . . . He will do a remarkable job . . . Once he begins speaking English, he will shock people . . . ," and so on. A host of people told me how proud Swamiji was of me. But one day, around Christmas, Swamiji called me, and contrary to what he conveyed through others, he said, "What's wrong with you? All day long, you hide yourself in your room. You have become a bookworm. This is not the way to learn. Spend time with others. I want you to learn American culture and the psychology of the people there. I want you to teach." Finally, Swamiji ended the conversation with a powerful command: "Don't behave like an arrogant brahmin!"

Thereafter, I started having more interaction with others. Instead of spending time improving my English, I joined the workforce at the Meditation Center—vacuuming, washing dishes, cooking, shoveling snow, running the mimeograph machine, and sealing envelopes. With my broken English and terrible accent, I started teaching courses on Sanskrit and the *Bhakti Sutras*.

Then one day, Swamiji telephoned me: "I am so disappointed that it has been almost three months that you have been in the States and still you are not doing anything." When I told him that I was teaching Sanskrit and the *Bhakti Sutras,* he shouted in a thundering voice, "Yes, I know. You are crawling at a snail's pace. I never thought you'd be such a disappointment to me!" and hung up.

A couple of months later, in the spring of 1980, Swamiji returned to the Institute's headquarters in Honesdale, Pennsylvania. I was already missing him very much, but when I heard that he was back in the States, I began to miss him even more. In the past three years, however, I had developed an instinct that told me when my interaction with him would not be an intrusion. Thus, despite the fact that I wanted to be with him, I hesitated to express my feelings to him. Two months passed after he returned from India. Neither he called me, nor I called him. In the middle of May, I began to receive his complaints secondhand: "After coming to the States, this boy has forgotten me. What can I do? He doesn't speak to me."

To me, his complaints were an indication that I should call or even visit him. But each time I called, his secretary told me that he was resting, or lecturing, or that he was simply not available. When I persisted, one day she told me that Swamiji wanted to know why I was calling and what I needed from him. It was obvious—he was ignoring me. A few times he told his secretary to tell me I was a nuisance and that I should stop behaving like a pest. But deep in my heart, I felt he was calling me. Finally one day, we connected. Before I could say anything, he said, "Why are you bothering me? What do you want from me?"

"I want to see you, Swamiji."

"Why?"

"Because," I replied, "it has been a long time since I have seen you."

"So what?"

"No, Swamiji, please give me your permission to see you."

At that, he shouted, "If you have already decided to see me, why do you need my permission?"

"Because it is not appropriate for me to come without asking."

His tone changed. "I have been dying to see you for all these months, and there you are sitting in Minnesota. Today, I am coming to Chicago. Come and see me there."

This is how I came to meet Swamiji in Chicago, and from there, came with him to the Institute's headquarters in Honesdale, Pennsylvania. Fortunately, before this incident I had learned that patience is the most important pre-requisite for learning from a master, for it is patience that serves as the ground for cultivating and maintaining a quiet mind. Patience helps us tap into the virtue of fortitude and enables us to keep trying in a graceful manner.

The first photo ever taken of Pandit Tigunait

Swami Rama of the Himalayas

The Power of Creative Intelligence

The evening that I arrived in Chicago, Swamiji was giving a public lecture. This was the first formal lecture by him that I had ever attended. It was being held in one of the Unity churches in downtown Chicago. Swamiji and I entered the hall. I took my seat in the back, and Swamiji walked up to the stage, folded his hands, bowed his head, and began to speak:

"I pray to the Divinity in you. The topic given to me this evening is 'Wave of Beauty and Wave of Bliss.' According to the sages of the Himalayas, beauty and bliss are inherent attributes of the Absolute. The Absolute Transcendental Reality is like an ocean of beauty, an ocean of bliss. The life force is like waves that continuously emerge from this ocean and subside in it. The entire world comes out of this beautiful, blissful Divine Being. After completing the cycle of its outward expansion, it dissolves again into the Divine Being. The purpose of life is to know that you are a wave of beauty and bliss. Just as waves in the ocean are not separate from the ocean, you are not separate from the beautiful and blissful Divine Being.

"You suffer from a sense of worthlessness because you do not know that you are a beautiful person. But you have an inherent urge to experience your inner beauty and joy. Not knowing how to turn your mind inward, you are trying to find beauty and joy in the external world. You have become dependent on others. When someone tells you that you are beautiful, your face lights up and you say, 'Thank you. You made my day.' You put on makeup, and when your sweetheart does not admire you, you feel terrible. Since you do not have the direct experience of that part of yourself which is beautiful, you look for confirmation from outside.

And when you don't find it, you are disappointed."

Swamiji went on speaking for almost thirty minutes. Then he said, "Now I'm open for questions and answers. Do you have any questions?"

Someone from the audience got up and asked, "What do you mean by inner beauty?"

In a booming voice, Swamiji replied, "There is a great scholar here who has done his Ph.D. on this very subject." He gestured to me and said, "Please get up." Hesitantly, I stood up. He asked me to come to the stage. My legs began to tremble. Hundreds of people were looking at me, and I felt as if I would collapse back into my seat. Then Swamiji spoke in Hindi, "*Chal, chal, chal* [come, come, come]." I don't remember how I managed to reach the stage or how the microphone came to be in my hand, but I spoke for ten or fifteen minutes. I have no idea what I said, but whatever it was, people seemed to understand it and like it. I have been lecturing ever since.

Later as I contemplated on this incident, I realized that we are blessed with infinite potentials. Lacking access to our inner dimensions we fail to know how rich we are. Thus, we suffer from a sense of inner poverty, causing us to feel that we are good-for-nothing. A teacher's job is to show us our own hidden wealth and to guide us to mine that wealth, using the tools and means that we call "spiritual techniques." The more we attenuate the sense of unworthiness and self-denigration, the more spontaneously and effortlessly our creative intelligence will begin to use our body, mind, and senses to express itself.

Pandit Tigunait in his first year in the United States

The Apple on the Coat Rack

A few days after I moved to the Institute headquarters in Pennsylvania, Swamiji appointed me as the spiritual director of the Institute. When I asked him what my duties were, he told me that I was in charge of maintaining discipline on campus. I had been in the United States for almost eight months. By that time I had learned that imposing discipline on Americans was not an easy task. I also knew that Americans could do anything provided they were motivated, but that this motivation had to come from within. Only then can discipline (which is key to self-transformation) be enjoyed; otherwise, discipline is just a form of torture.

The Himalayan Institute is a spiritual organization, and everyone is expected to be loving and kind, not to interfere in others' lives, and to carry a sweet smile in all situations and circumstances. I knew that I had been appointed spiritual director not only by Swami Rama, the "kind saint," but also by Swami Rama, "the disciplinarian." I had to figure out how to measure up to the expectations of both. I tried my best and made some headway, even though I knew I had not fully mastered the art of managing people. But when I asked Swamiji to elaborate on what he meant by discipline, all he said was, "You are not a child any more. You know it very well. It is time to figure out how to put your knowledge into practice."

One day, Swamiji was walking through the central corridor of the Institute's main building. He stopped at the back door and shouted, "Get Panditji!" When I arrived, he pointed to an apple that had been left on the coat rack and roared, "Is this how you are maintaining discipline? People are leaving apples and cups and plates all over the building!"

For the next several days, whenever he saw me, Swamiji brought up this issue and asked me if I had found any solution to this apple business. I knew that the apple on the coat rack was only an excuse to teach me a lesson that was too big to be taught in a classroom setting. So I told him, "Swamiji, I am still trying to find the solution, and I am sure that with your help, soon I will find it."

With a mischievous look, he said, "Let me tell you about one of my experiences. I had a student. He was an educated and intelligent man. He practiced his hatha yoga and breathing exercises for several hours a day. He was an excellent teacher of hatha yoga and natural health, but he always complained that he had a scattered mind and therefore could not meditate for more than five minutes. I observed his interactions with others and could not find any flaw in him, for he was kind and considerate, always ready to help others. So I visited him at his home. He had a big house, but there was no room in it even to walk. From his shoe rack all the way to his living room, bedroom, kitchen, and bathroom, you had to walk carefully lest you bump into things and break your toes, or even your teeth. Then I realized how careless and disorganized he was within—this was reflected so vividly in his external life."

Then Swamiji concluded, "Just as the unkempt atmosphere of this gentleman's house was a reflection of his mind, this apple is a reflection of someone's carelessness. It is clearly a symptom of a disorganized and scattered mind. Such people are bound to miss their practice, keep hopping from one task to another, or waste their time gossiping. Carelessness causes people to be sloppy, both in their inner and outer worlds. Discipline and sloppiness do not go together."

To initiate a true process of self-transformation, first you have to discipline yourself. Discipline means overcoming your carelessness. To start and complete any kind of task, spiritual or mundane, you have to organize your external and internal life. You can do so only when you are not careless. Sloth, inertia, procrastination, and all other negative tendencies receive their nourishment from one main fountain—carelessness.

Reality Lifts Its Veil

Soon after I arrived in Pennsylvania, I began to see the drama that goes on in any community that tries to achieve a common goal while juggling the different values, philosophies, and personality traits its members bring with them.

One of the Institute's board members was a rich man who had donated a large sum of money to the Institute. Although he did not live on campus, he played an active role in the Institute's functioning. Due to his wealth, closeness to Swamiji, and apparent spiritual aspiration, he exerted a great deal of power and influence on the community. I found him arrogant but I thought, "Who am I to judge?" I was the newest addition to the community and I had not yet become fully familiar with how things worked. Therefore, when I found anything odd in this gentleman, I simply ignored it. If his behavior disturbed the Institute's atmosphere, I tried to bring things back to normal by infusing the atmosphere with friendliness, thus preventing the situation from turning into a big issue.

One day, this man's daughter became ill and he made an appointment for her at the Institute's clinic. When the girl did not appear for her appointment, the doctor called his home to check on her. The man answered and gave the doctor a tongue-lashing, accusing him of negligence, insisting that he should have made a house call instead of a telephone call. The doctor was astonished and deeply hurt.

When Swamiji heard about this incident, he took strong action: he dismissed the man from the board and denied him further access to the Institute. This created a big commotion. Some residents felt relief; others felt that Swamiji should have shown patience and compassion. Within a matter of a few months, Swamiji and the Institute became the target of a barrage of accusations and lawsuits. In my dual capacity as spiritual director and Swamiji's student, I watched how months later this episode was still draining away time, energy, and money. Many people, not only here at headquarters, but throughout the country, were still gossiping about it. I wondered, "If such an abrupt and harsh action on Swamiji's part was really necessary, couldn't it have been handled more diplomatically?"

One day, I expressed these feelings to Swamiji. He said, "The Institute is an ashram. Here, people are supposed to live in peace and harmony. Love and discipline are the foundation of ashram life. A superiority complex and sense of self-importance destroy the peace in family, community, and society. An ashram is a place where you come and get complete rest. It is not a place for socializing, nor is it a place for debating philosophical or religious issues. And it is certainly not a place for politics. Self-discipline and self-analysis are the grounds for ashram life.

"You come to an ashram to learn, to practice yoga; and then you return to the larger world to test how far you have progressed on the spiritual path," Swamiji continued. "If you wish to become a permanent ashramite, it is the duty of the teacher to lead you through the fire. Blessed are those who endure the heat, for one day, they shine and give light to the world. An ashram without a disciplined teacher and inspired students is just like any other community."

After a few days of contemplating on this, I expressed my thoughts to Swamiji. "Swamiji, it seems to me that this place is lacking a clear-cut identity. It is caught between being an ashram and an educational institution. The same is true with you. Some think that you are a great master and others view you as head of an educational organization. Those who think of you as a great master worship you and spiritualize your every word and move, regardless of how mundane. Others, however, see your actions as politically incorrect, arrogant, and irrational. You are established in yourself. You may take such situations as mere drama, but those who are not like you take these dramas for real. To prevent such complications, people should know whether the Himalayan Institute is an ashram or an educational entity just like any other college or university. Without making this distinction clear, if you put someone through fire, there will be hundreds putting you on fire."

Swamiji laughed and said, "Sonny, you have caught hold of the spirit of the modern world. Since now you know that the forces governing a spiritual institution are the same as those that govern the rest of the world, you will not be disappointed when reality lifts its veil."

"Please do not ignore my question," I pleaded. "Is this Institute an ashram or an educational entity?"

Swamiji answered, "Right now, it is both. When it becomes big, shrink it to an ashram."

For a long time, I pondered why all great seekers and adepts in the world preferred to live in solitude. I realized that collective consciousness of a community far exceeds the power and charisma of any individual, regardless of how enlightened that individual is. An enlightened master can initially create an atmosphere conducive to self-transformation, but it is the combined effort of both the leader and all the members of the community that helps maintain that atmosphere.

Unfortunately, the mob mentality that propels the wheel of politics also casts its spell on aspirants who are not vigilant and focused on their goal. Because the majority of aspirants is not vigilant and not focused on the goal, it is difficult to maintain a community of any size without spending a great deal of time cleaning up the mess.

Therefore, we must figure out how to shrink a spiritual organization when it becomes big. As I learned from Swamiji, this can be done by separating all business activities, including those which are educational and humanitarian in nature, from activities which are purely spiritual. The former activities focus on business, and the latter on self-discipline. Like any other business, a spiritual organization must exercise a high level of discipline in compliance with moral and ethical business standards. By doing so, the business runs well. However, it takes away the organization's main focus—spiritual discipline and practice. If you don't pay attention, then within no time, a spiritual organization can turn into a business entity. That is a big loss. But if you are vigilant and keep the mission in focus, then you will be able to maintain the peaceful atmosphere which is necessary for personal growth. Do not measure the growth and success of a spiritual organization by looking at how large a following it has gathered.

A Liar Exposed

Every year, the Himalayan Institute offered a silence retreat to its long-term students, teachers, faculty, and directors. During one of those retreats, Swamiji made a comment that he was not able to teach some of the meditative techniques that are unique to his tradition. When people asked what the problem was, he said, "You people have holes in your heads."

One of the faculty members asked Swamiji, "How can we seal those holes?"

"First, you have to know what those holes are, and how those holes were made in the first place. Then you can figure out how to seal them," Swamiji responded.

Everyone present had his or her own interpretation. I wanted to pin down mine. One evening, when the opportunity presented itself, I put my question before Swamiji. In response he said, "It doesn't matter. You know that I love you." This answer did not satisfy me. I kept pressing. Finally, he said, "Son, you are in the habit of lying."

I was shocked. I went back in time trying to remember an incident when I had lied. I could not recollect even one. Finally, after prolonged contemplation, I concluded that during my lectures I tell stories, and if the stories are not based on facts, then by telling them, I am lying. When I relayed my finding to Swamiji, he said, "No, that is not called lying, for by telling such stories you are simply trying to make your point. Contemplate more and be vigilant in your thoughts, speech, and actions. Then you will see how you lie."

A few months passed. One day, there was a slide show in the auditorium. A group of people from the Institute had gone to India and brought back with them a large number of slides of the places they had visited in the

Himalayas. During the slide show, people from the audience kept asking the tour leader to identify the places on the screen. Quite often, she asked me to help her. Whenever I explained the history and spiritual significance of these places, I noticed a great deal of excitement from the audience, but when I did not, they seemed disappointed. Just because I was from India, and because a large part of the Himalayas are in India, people assumed I knew everything about these mountains. What they did not know was that the Himalayas are the largest mountain range in the world, and it is not possible for a person to know everything about them. I could not bear their disappointment in me. So, to make them happy, I made all efforts to give a commentary on the slides, even if it meant using the information I had read in books.

My general knowledge of the tour's destination points in the Himalayas gave me enough latitude to describe with probability: "It looks like such and such place," and so on. Inspired by people's enthusiastic response to my commentary, I gradually became more affirmative in my tone. I made statements that this is such and such place, and when I did not see anyone from the audience contradicting me, I went ahead describing the spiritual significance of the place on the basis of what I knew from books and folk tales.

By the time I was at the peak of sharing my knowledge, a statue of a god appeared on the screen. This statue is located at one of the holy sites of the Himalayas known as Joshimath. I had not been to Joshimath and had never seen this statue. But this particular place and the statue are of great importance as they are at the heart of one of the four most significant Hindu pilgrimage sites. I knew enough about this place to astonish those sitting in the audience. While giving my commentary, I brought in the elements of history, culture, philosophy, and mythology, and adding the folk tale I said, "See how the arm of the statue is so thin? According to local belief, this arm is getting thinner every day. The day it becomes disconnected from the statue's torso, two of the mountain peaks beyond this site will collapse, and the trail leading to the shrine of Badrinath will become blocked forever. Badrinath will no longer be accessible to humankind."

At this, someone from the audience exclaimed with excitement, "Panditji, have you been there?"

"Oh, yes!" I said spontaneously.

Soon after the slide show, we did our evening prayer and everyone dispersed. As was my daily routine, after the evening prayer, I visited Swamiji in his room. I knocked on his door. In response, there came a low and drawn-out voice: "Come in." I entered the room. There I saw Swamiji reclining on his couch, eyes closed. Sensing that I had entered, he opened his eyes slightly and said, "So, great Pandit, when did you go to Joshimath?" and then closed his eyes again.

I almost died of embarrassment. It seemed as if the energy from my body totally drained out. I couldn't stand on my feet. I sat down on the floor. Thereafter, Swamiji did not say a word. The liar in me sat in front of him fully exposed. After five minutes, unable to remain in his company, I got up and murmured, "Swamiji, I think I should leave now."

Without the slightest movement in the rest of his body, he opened his eyes, looked at me with pity, and closed them again. As he did so, his unspoken words reverberated in every cell of my being: "You liar, who cares whether you stay or leave?"

The next day, when we met, Swamiji made a brief comment: "Gain maturity in your speech and actions. You can do that when your thought process is guided by the faculty of discrimination. Thoughts motivate speech, and the content of speech decides the course of action. If you are not aware of yourself at the level of your thoughts, you will not have control over your tongue. A person careless in thought is bound to have a sloppy tongue. A sloppy tongue doesn't care what it speaks. That is why even when you don't mean to lie, you do it carelessly."

Keep Your Ears Plugged

Once my master gave me a practice. At face value, it sounded very simple. In fact, it was so simple, straightforward, and easy that my mind hardly registered it. The core of the practice was comprised of remembering a mantra while focusing my mind at the center between the eyebrows. It was supposed to be done in the corpse pose—lying on one's back. After Swamiji finished explaining how to arrange auxiliary practices around the main practice, he said, "Make sure that during this practice, you keep your ears plugged. Also make sure that you don't do this practice for more than thirty minutes. If in the middle of the practice you fall asleep, do not start it again; wait until the next day."

I chose 6:30 in the morning as the time for this practice. I completed it without falling asleep or without any distraction. It was very peaceful. The second day it was even more peaceful. The third day, it was so peaceful and delightful that all day long I felt like I was surfing the ocean of bliss.

The fourth day, within a matter of a minute or so, I slipped into such a quiet state of mind that I could hear the sound of my heartbeat. It became annoying. As I focused my mind with greater intensity at the center between the eyebrows, I succeeded in withdrawing the mind from hearing my heartbeat. Then the cotton ball that I was using as an earplug turned into a nuisance. The fibers of the cotton were tickling inside my ear, and it seemed as if they were moving, creating an unbearable sound. I tried my best to withdraw my mind from that sensation, but to no avail. Then I thought, "Well, earplugs are for those beginners who are distracted by external sounds. I'm an experienced meditator—

Pandit Tigunait's family

Pandit Tigunait's extended family

Pandit Tigunait and his wife, Meera

227

I'll take them out. Why struggle with the sound created by the fibers of these cotton balls?"

I removed the cotton balls from my ears. It felt very good. Now, without earplugs, I reached the same meditative state that I had reached the previous day, and ten minutes later, I even went a step beyond. It was an amazing experience. I was able to feel that I had a body, but it occupied just a tiny corner of my consciousness. I was awestruck with the wonder of knowing that I had a body but I was not the body.

In those days, I lived in one of the rooms on the second floor of the Institute's main building. There were more than forty rooms on the wing where I lived. At the peak of my practice, I sensed someone walking in the corridor. For a few seconds, I was able to ignore it. Suddenly, my focus shattered when I heard a thundering sound coming from the corridor. It was someone's footsteps. In the realm of my inner awareness, this sound was so explosive that it blew away my body consciousness. On one hand, I was still able to see my body lying on the floor of my room, but I could not feel it. On the other hand, I felt an excruciating pain in the subtle body that hung over the physical one. My internal faculty of perception was still intact and showed me clearly that the life force moving back and forth between the physical and subtle bodies was damaged by the sudden explosive sound. As soon as I understood that my breath was not moving in my physical body, a realization dawned: I am dead. This realization terrified me. In the field of consciousness that still filled the room and the whole wing on the second floor, I experienced pain beyond the capacity of the nervous system and brain to contain.

I looked at my wife sleeping in bed. I remembered that just a few months ago I had gotten married. I began thinking, "What will happen to her if I never come back to life? How are my elderly parents and young sisters going to withstand the shock of my death? Oh my God—I'm really dead!" The recollection of my wife, parents, and sisters, and my attachment to them, intensified my pain to the point that I began to cry loudly. Yet, in the midst of this painful experience, it was thrilling to know that there was no pain in the physical body. I thought of waking my wife, hoping she might be able to help bring me into my body. I shook her and shouted loudly to awaken her. That's when I realized that I was doing this with my non-physical body. This realization further added to my misery. Then a thought flashed: "This whole thing happened during my practice. Had I not removed the cotton balls from my ears, this external sound would not have hit me so hard." I also remembered that this practice had been given to me by Swamiji. At this recollection, I saw Swamiji as if he had just walked through the door.

In the vision, he entered the room, furious, and yelled at me, "I told you to keep your ears plugged!" Then his face changed. Looking at me kindly, he said, "But it doesn't matter." He stretched his hands toward the ceiling where I had been feeling the greatest concentration of my consciousness. As he lowered his hands toward my physical body lying on the floor, I felt myself entering it. Then he disappeared.

I regained my body consciousness. I felt that it was my body and I was in it. Still, I was not able to move it. It was numb. Then a thought flashed: "Was I dreaming? Did I fall asleep during my practice today? Did the breath of life really become disconnected? Right now, am I still dreaming?" By this time, with effort, I was able to move my toes and fingers. I worked hard. I stretched my arms and legs, and got up; however, I was still feeling weak. Holding onto the bed, I walked to my wife and woke her up. Wanting to confirm whether it had been an out-of-body experience or just a dream, I asked my wife, "Meera, was I crying?" When she said no, I concluded that this experience was neither a dream nor a hallucination.

Normally, people think that the more difficult the practice, the more advanced. From this experience, I learned that a simple, straightforward practice can open the door to the inner dimension of life, provided we do not distort it. It took generations to discover, refine, and then systematize such simple but powerful practices, and it is important that we do not become too creative while doing these practices.

A Debilitating Disease

My master had a disciple. He was a very learned and well-traveled person. His retentive power and knowledge of scriptures were extraordinary. He was a highly acclaimed teacher, a proponent of Hindu scriptures, and a social reformer. When I met him for the first time, I was impressed with his profound knowledge and his respect for Swamiji, and I was thankful to Providence for blessing me with a spiritual brother who was senior to me in every respect.

Once a year, he visited the Institute's headquarters, and his visit always created a great stir among the students and faculty. Some eagerly awaited receiving his love, blessings, and guidance. Others, however, sought every excuse to stay away from him and prayed that he would leave soon. In those days, there were a number of Ph.D.s and M.D.s on the Institute's faculty. Hardly any of them liked him. I was very new to this country. Just as with everything else, I was trying to understand why Swamiji's students, the residents of the Institute, and the faculty members reacted to this man's presence in such diverse ways. Personally, I was happy to have him with us, for to me he was a walking encyclopedia on almost every subject. In my capacity as spiritual director, faculty, and board member, however, I felt it was important that I know his background and his place in the Institute's history. Everything I gathered from the students was positive and inspiring. But some faculty members commented: "He lives in his own world. He is arrogant." After my repeated questions, Swamiji remarked, "He's a hypocrite. He exploits my name."

Several years passed, and my perception of this man began to change. I saw him speak and act in a manner that defied the standards and values of any tradition. He com-

pared his students with the obvious intention of engender-
ing inferiority complexes in them. He prescribed disciplines that students likely could not follow, and when they
did not measure up to his expectations, he would skillfully
prove that they lacked sincerity, willpower, and true desire
to achieve enlightenment. Then he would further impress
and oblige them by pouring out his so-called teacherly love
and compassion.

For a while, I did not have a reason to involve myself in
what went on between him and his students. Nevertheless,
this melodrama forced me to reflect on why such a learned
person would treat his students in a manner that is coun-
terproductive to the spiritual growth of both himself and
his students. A little later, however, I was put in a situation
where I had no choice but to involve myself in my brother
disciple's teaching tactics.

As my role of spiritual director became established,
people's trust in me as a spiritual guide grew tremendously.
My position encouraged them to seek my advice with the
underlying assumption that it would be more authoritative
and conclusive than the instructions they had received
from other teachers trained by Swami Rama. This assumption put me in a very odd situation. My position demanded that I offer my spiritual counseling to them and
that I do it with honesty and sincerity.

Then my skill as a teacher was put to the test. One day,
my brother disciple gave a lecture. During this session, he
emphasized the importance of doing meditation regularly.
At the end of his lecture, someone asked him, "What happens when you sometimes miss your meditation practice?"

He answered, "When you miss your practice by one
day, you go backward by one lifetime." The audience found
this very discouraging. In the course of answering other
questions, he made a big deal of doing one's practice at ex-

actly the same time and in the same place, in the same sitting position with the same mala beads, while wearing the same robe, and so on. Then, quoting one of the scriptures, he said, "The best time to meditate is between twelve and three in the night. The next best time is between three and six in the morning. Blessed are those who keep their body, mind, and soul fully yoked in supreme consciousness from midnight to six. The nectar you receive and drink during these hours of meditation will remove the soul's hunger forever." Then, rolling his eyes as though they were brimming with the nectar he himself had gathered the night before, he said, while pointing to himself, "That is how this sleepless speck of pollen belonging to the lotus feet of my master spends his nights, and as you know, goes on dispensing the aroma of the long lineage of Himalayan sages to all those who deserve to rejoice in it."

The audience was spellbound. Some felt they were fortunate to be studying with this great man, and others felt they were not qualified to learn anything from him because they were far from being able to spend their nights in meditation. After the lecture was over, a number of people, one by one, bombarded me with their questions. All I could do was answer them as diplomatically as possible.

Later, during a private conversation, I asked my brother disciple, "Do you really remain awake the whole night and spend your time between midnight and six in meditation?"

With indescribable sincerity, he said, "Pandit Rajmaniji, if I say yes, I'll be boasting. If I say no, I'll be lying. Therefore, you tell me, should I say yes or no?" This answer threw me. I knew his routine quite well. It was true that he worked the graveyard shift—he did his correspondence in the middle of the night, called his favorite students at three in the morning to tell them that it was their meditation time, and called overseas where it was daytime.

Then he would go to bed when everyone else was starting their day.

When I expressed my discomfort about him to Swamiji, he said, "Just as the body has a spine, spiritual life has a spine. You can sit and walk comfortably only when you have a straight spine. Similarly, you can complete your spiritual journey safely and comfortably when the spine of your spiritual life is straight. And do you know what is the spine of spirituality? Truthfulness. Hypocrisy is such a debilitating disease that it consumes the spiritual energy that you generate through your *tapas* [austere disciplines]. Then the spine of spirituality—truthfulness—caves in. Remember this."

Blessings That Don't Bear Fruit

On the Institute's 400-acre campus, there are certain spots so beautiful and peaceful that once there you automatically slip into a state of deep contemplation. One such spot is located at the northeastern part of the campus. Residents call this area "Sound of Music Hill." At dawn and dusk, the Sound of Music Hill uncovers its unique beauty. Regardless of the season, here in the warmth of this beauty, you will melt. Then, whether your consciousness flows toward nirvana or romance depends on the contents of your mind. This is where residents and guests fall in love and decide the course of their destiny.

One summer, a couple decided to get married. They chose the Sound of Music Hill for the ceremony. I performed the wedding. Following the injunctions of the Vedic tradition I concluded the ceremony and gave my blessings; then everyone came forward to congratulate the couple. Both the bride and bridegroom had known me for a long time, and for the past several years they had been my students. I had great love and affection for them. Once they finished greeting their friends and well-wishers, they came to me and, in a purely Indian style, touched my feet and said, "We seek your special blessings. To us, this is not just a marriage; it is the beginning of our spiritual life."

I knew their request was genuine and sincere. I was touched by their humility and love for me. With great joy, I put my hands on their heads and showered my blessings. My blessings included the promise of complete fulfillment: health, wealth, happiness, self-realization in this lifetime, and much more.

Then the party moved from the Sound of Music Hill to the Institute's dining hall, where the wedding reception was being held. Accompanied by a group of people, mostly the Institute's residents, I walked toward the dining hall. On the way, we came upon Swamiji. After his customary remarks—How are you? What are you doing?—he focused his eyes on me and spoke loudly, "How are you, Funeral Director? Did you ever count how many times you have performed such funerals?"

Everyone, including myself, was bewildered by Swamiji's remarks. Some tried to handle their bewilderment with laughter and others simply remained quiet. I tried to understand why, on this auspicious occasion, Swamiji called me a funeral director. The part of his remark, "Did you ever count how many times you have performed such funerals?" was especially puzzling. The whole day I pondered on this funeral director issue, but could not arrive at any conclusion.

In the evening, I asked him, "Swamiji, I have not been able to figure out how I became a funeral director, and whose funeral I have been performing."

Swamiji replied, "Due to your foolishness, you have been performing your own funerals. When are you going to get rid of your sloppy tongue? So easily, you still become victim of your emotions."

I sat there before him, trying to understand his comments and how they related to performing my own funeral. Finally, I gave up and asked humbly, "Swamiji, I feel pitiful for having such a dense mind. I have not been able to understand this funeral business."

Swamiji responded, "You become excited when you see people acknowledging you as a spiritually evolved soul. This excitement creates an inner unrest. You begin to believe that you really are a very evolved soul and you become attached to this recognition. You allow yourself to believe it is true. Then, not wanting to discover the validity of this belief, you respond to people in compliance with their acknowledgement.

"The blessings you showered this morning on the newlywed couple were motivated by the thrill of being acknowledged as a great and pious soul. You showered your blessings: "May you be healthy, wealthy, and prosperous, and attain enlightenment in this lifetime." You can give something only when you have it in the first place. You can't give what you don't have. Did you ever assess your ability to grant such boons? If you keep making such promises without knowing whether or not you can ever fulfill them, then what will happen? The inner intelligence will circulate a silent message throughout creation that you are a careless person, a harmless liar, and thus, not to be trusted. That is when your blessings do not bear any fruit. You turn into a perfunctory priest with sweet-sounding but empty words."

Then with a big laugh Swamiji said, "Those who don't understand my point are reborn as drums with only one function—to produce a good sound upon receiving beatings. Watch out, my son."

The Flame
in the Cave

How Not to Be Born as a Dog

In October of 1996, I was writing a book, *From Death to Birth*. Deborah Willoughby, the editor of *Yoga International* magazine, took the lead in putting together the manuscript: she took dictation, edited the text, and finally polished the language. When the book was only partially written, we heard that Swamiji was not well. So, wishing to spend time with him, Deborah and I went to India, taking the manuscript with us. We stayed at Swamiji's ashram in Rishikesh, but, due to his health, he was staying on the campus of the Himalayan Institute Hospital in Dehra Dun, fifteen miles from the ashram. We spent every morning writing the book and visited Swamiji in the afternoons.

Swamiji was suffering from end-stage cancer and was getting weaker every day. Most of the time, he was resting in bed. But all of a sudden, late one morning, he opened his eyes and said, "You know, Panditji knows how not to be born as a dog!" The people attending him were bewildered, for they did not understand the context in which Swamiji made this statement. When they asked him what he meant, he briefly told them the story of the dog that came to the court of Lord Rama seeking justice, and indicated that I would elaborate if they asked me.

Swami Rama with Pandit Tigunait's son, Ishan

That afternoon, when I visited the hospital, one of Swamiji's students asked me to tell her the story in detail. I was surprised because I had dictated this story for my book that same morning. The context in which I told it was, "As we sow, so shall we reap." This is a simple and straightforward law: We harvest the crop that we have planted. Nature provides conditions that are conducive to the growth of the crop, but to a great extent we have freedom of choice in deciding what we wish to plant. God is the creator of this world, but not of our destiny. To clarify the point, I had told the following story from one of the ancient scriptures:

There once lived a brahmin in the kingdom of Lord Rama. Although poor and illiterate, he was known for his piety. His practice of austerity consisted of bathing several times a day, covering his body with a meager amount of clothing, owning nothing, living only on alms, and reciting scriptures. One morning, as was his daily routine, he set out to beg for alms, walking on a path so narrow that only one person could pass at a time. And there on the trail he happened upon an old dog. The pious brahmin assumed that the dog would give way, but without paying any attention, it continued to rest. Irritated, the brahmin hurled his staff and hit the dog's head. Panicked, the dog jumped off the trail, cried for a while, and then dragged his frail and wounded body to the gate of Lord Rama's palace. There he spoke in human tongue, asking the guards to help him reach Lord Rama so that he could seek justice from this noble king. The dog's ability to speak in human tongue caught the guards' interest, and thus he was brought to the court.

When Rama asked what his complaint was, the dog cried, "Sir, I am an old, frail dog. I was resting on a trail, and without any warning a brahmin hit me on the head with his staff. I seek justice from your court."

Lord Rama summoned the brahmin, and when he arrived, Rama asked him what he had to say in his defense. The brahmin acknowledged the fact that he had hit the dog. When asked why he did it, he said, "Sir, because of my hunger, I was irritable. Furthermore, I did not know any better."

Rama asked his council to help him decide the brahmin's punishment, and every member of the council said, "So far, we have been dealing with disputes between humans. This is an extraordinary case. Your Majesty alone can judge its weight and grant the appropriate justice."

So Rama said to the dog, "You do not seem to be an ordinary dog. Please help me decide a punishment proportionate to the degree of the offense. What kind of punishment do you wish this brahmin to receive?"

"Punishment does not depend on the wishes of the plaintiff," the dog replied. "However, if you appoint me to your council for the time being, I will advise you to appoint him the spiritual head of the grand and prestigious monastery of Kalinjar. That should be his punishment."

"Be it so," Lord Rama declared. And thereafter, following the customs of that monastery, the brahmin was given a ceremonial bath, a fancy robe befitting his new position, a gold-plated staff, and was mounted on an elephant so that he could proceed to his monastery.

As soon as the brahmin departed, the court was adjourned. But as the advisers and courtiers, including the dog, were about to leave, Lord Rama pointed at the dog and said, "Everyone is puzzled by this verdict. People are wondering whether the appointment of this brahmin as the head of such a prestigious and religious institution is a punishment or a reward."

"Your Majesty," the dog replied, "it is the most terrible punishment one can imagine."

"Explain why," Lord Rama said.

The dog responded, "Your Majesty, this brahmin is ignorant, arrogant, and hungry for name, fame, and popularity. He has no control over his urges. He is easily overcome by anger, and that means he is full of unfulfilled desires. As a beggar, all he has received in his life is humiliation, which he has been hiding under the garb of non-possessiveness and humility. But as soon as he assumes his new position, he will be hailed as a holy man—a liaison between humans and God. He will not be able to assimilate this honor, and very soon he will suffer from religious constipation. He will insult people; he will oppress them. He will make so many mistakes that he will be punished by his own karma."

Rama asked, "But how do you know all of these things?"

Holding his head in his paws, the dog gave a deep sigh and said, "Because, My Lord, one day I was the head of that institution."

As I finished dictating this story to Deborah for my book *From Death to Birth,* I said, "Deborah, you are the president of the Himalayan Institute, and I am the spiritual head. If, due to our negligence, the teachings of the sages are distorted at the Institute, both of us will be born as dogs!" This was the exact time when Swamiji, lying in his bed at the hospital site, made his sudden remark, "You know, Panditji knows how not to be born as a dog."

The scriptures say, "Pigs' droppings are as good as name, fame, and honor; being hailed as a guru is mere noise; ego is another form of drunkenness. Only after renouncing these three does one truly remember the name of God." Self-transformation is the main objective of any form of spiritual practice. In the process of self-transformation, it is important that we reflect on our internal states. While external trappings may give the illusory appearance of holiness, it is self-reflection that enables us to recognize our strengths and weaknesses. Self-reflection can tell us whether we are practicing beggary in the name of religion (and in the process, darkening our minds with self-humiliation), or if we are practicing non-possessiveness and letting our hearts shine with true humility. Without self-reflection, we fail to see and acknowledge the truth. We embrace the delusion that we are holy men—liaisons between humans and God—and at that point, we are doomed. A fate even worse ensues when we cast our magic spell of delusion over others.

Grounded

As Swamiji neared the last days of his life, his words became increasingly brief and precise. One day, when I walked into his room, he inquired if I wanted to ask him anything. I told him that in regard to working for his mission, I had a general idea of what I should be doing, but I wondered whether he had specific instructions for me. He said, "Yes. Serve the sages." I tried to understand the implication of his response, but when I could not, I asked him what he meant. He uttered a second sentence, "It means you are grounded."

Now I was even more puzzled. Regarding the first statement, I could assume that serving the sages meant translating scriptures and offering seminars and courses on subjects that would infuse human hearts with love and compassion. I also assumed it meant mobilizing the Institute's resources to serve humanity, just as he had. But the second statement defeated all my assumptions and inferences. When I put my bewilderment before him, he spoke his third sentence with even more impenetrable meaning, "You are not allowed to watch boxing, let alone participate in it."

"Today, I am too slow, Swamiji," I said. "Please help me."

"It simply means," Swamiji answered, "do not involve yourself in any religion. Religious leaders all over the world have turned into boxers. Remember, you don't shine by defacing others. Boxing is a painful sport, and I wish humanity would replace it with something better. You have no role in boxing. You are a gatekeeper at the cave of the heart. You are a faithful envoy of the sages, and as such, your job is to attend the flame that shines eternally on the altar of the heart."

Sages do not belong to any caste, creed, nation, or ethnic group. They love this world and everything that exists in it, because this world is God's creation and the creator resides in every part of it. Creation is the manifest form of the creator. Serving creation is serving the Lord of Life, who loves this world so much. Fortunate are those who are confined to the cave of the heart, with no power or privilege to perpetuate misery in this world. And even more fortunate are those who dedicate their lives to serving the flame that shines eternally in the inner chamber of all living beings.

age, does anyone pause to explore the possibility of using the cumulative knowledge of our forefathers to enrich our present and guide us into the future? We are concerned about preserving our heritage, even though most of the time we know nothing or very little about it. This is a great loss. The more we know about the essence of our heritage, the greater respect we will have for it.

The greater our respect for our own heritage, I realized, the greater our respect for the traditions of others, whether or not we know much about them. But instead of examining our roots, we choose to believe our heritage is superior to others out of sheer vanity. The truth is that people in all times and places have worked hard to discover the tools and means to live a healthy, happy life. They have preserved their discoveries in philosophy, mythology, religious practices, literature, music, dance, and the other arts. When we find a way to tap into these sources, we will understand what our individual potentials are, how to unfold them, and how to attain freedom from fear without becoming a source of fear to others.

The Flame in the Cave

On November 13, I was in New Delhi. At around 11:30 that night, I received a telephone call from Prem Sobte, the manager of Swamiji's ashram, informing me that Swamiji had left his body. I immediately hired a taxi and returned to the Himalayan Institute Hospital, where Swamiji had taken his last breath. We arrived the next morning and went straight to his room, where his body was lying on the bed. With my eyes closed, I stood silently before him, for to me this was a time to bring his teachings into practice and to internalize my living guide. After a few minutes, I suggested to the others present that we change his clothes and lay the body on the floor in a room where people could come and offer their homage.

But getting a new set of clothes was not so easy. Overnight, a rash of mistrust had arisen among the core group of people who attended Swamiji during the last phase of his life. They were already locked in a dispute over who was the most senior student and who could be trusted with Swamiji's valuables. And what were those valuables? Rosary beads, thought to be the icon of Swamiji's spiritual powers. A gigantic *rudraksha* bead, which people had come to believe was a living Shiva. A large emerald in the form of a Shiva lingam that had recently appeared in Swamiji's living room. To some, this emerald Shiva lingam was special because it had come from Swamiji's cave monastery; to others, it was special because it was worth a lot of money.

These students were afraid of each other, but they were even more afraid of Mohit Kumar, Swamiji's biological son. Mohit was on his way back from a shrine deep in the Himalayas, where he had gone to undertake a practice of intense austerity to propitiate Shiva for Swamiji's recovery.

He was expected at any moment. Even though it had been three or four decades since Swamiji had left his family and re-entered monastic life, those in positions of authority here in India feared that, at this critical moment, giving Swamiji's family members access to his belongings would have undesirable consequences. So, before Mohit could return from his retreat, they made sure that all the doors were locked and Swamiji's belongings were secured. Furthermore, there were several locks with a different person holding the key to each one, so getting a new robe for him took some time.

Since early that morning people from all walks of life had been flocking to the campus for a last glimpse of this great man. There were many dignitaries, among them the governor of the state, cabinet ministers from the central government, and prominent religious leaders. Mohit had arrived by now, and most of these VIPs sought him out to offer their condolences. That threatened those in positions of authority at the hospital. To my amazement, even some of Swamiji's closest disciples were so frantic over this development that they asked me to join them in strategizing a way to prevent Mohit from gaining credibility as Swamiji's successor.

The cremation was scheduled to take place in Haridwar on the afternoon of the 15th, and that is when the drama reached its climax. By now, tens of thousands of people were milling around the campus, waiting to join the funeral procession; the national media was there with cameras and microphones. The body was laid on a bed of flowers resting on a motorized chariot. Now the question was, who would have the honor of officially attending Swamiji's body? According to Indian tradition, the closest family member has the honor of accompanying the body and lighting the pyre. When the deceased is a householder, normally this honor goes to the oldest son; when he is a swami, it goes to his successor or, in the successor's absence, to the monk next in the order of seniority. After putting up stiff resistance, the Himalayan Institute Hospital Trust finally allowed Mohit to be among those who accompanied the body on its final journey.

The procession moved slowly, stopping occasionally at ashrams along the way, where groups of saints and their students offered flowers and garlands as a token of their regard for Swamiji. It took hours to reach the cremation ground. The traditional caretakers of the burning ghat had prepared a pyre of sandalwood logs on the bank of the Ganga. The body was ceremonially transferred to the pyre and the fire lit. I stood near the pyre, lost in my own world of thoughts and emotions, reflecting on how everyone—great or small, learned or ignorant—leaves this world. This reality is so clear, and yet we busy ourselves with trivial tasks. Without any effort on my part, the past was slipping into the present. The twenty years I spent with Swamiji flashed before me, and as I watched in my mind, I saw so many scenes of our time together.

Suddenly one of Swamiji's partially consumed legs separated from the rest of the body and fell from the pyre. Without hesitation, the caretaker flipped it back into the flames with a long bamboo pole. My eyes refused to see the foot I had massaged so many times being consumed by the fire. Instead, amidst the dazzling flames, I saw this great soul, clothed in his radiant body, walking regally down the hall at the Institute in Pennsylvania. I saw him standing at the podium and heard him greeting his students with the familiar phrase, "I pray to the Divinity within you." Then the scene shifted to a summer lawn, Swamiji surrounded by children, asking them, "Who loves you the most?" And the children chorusing, "Baba!" Then he turned to the parents, "Give your undivided love and attention to these blossoms. This is how you will serve God."

Immersed in these memories, with the flames filling the cave of my heart, I barely heard a voice ask, "Pandit Rajmaniji, may I talk to you privately?" I turned to see one of Swamiji's senior disciples addressing me. We walked a short distance from the flames, and then this gentleman said, "Pandit Rajmaniji, when Sri Swamiji was in his body he made all the decisions, including how to allocate funds for different charitable activities, especially the money that came from love offerings. Have you decided what we are going to do with the love offerings that students make when they get their mantra initiation?"

I was stunned—it felt like an entire mountain had dropped on my chest. Here the body of the teacher was not yet consumed by fire and the students were worried about how to distribute the love offerings among themselves. I had seen human beings falling into disgraceful behavior before, but not until that moment did I realize how thoroughly greed can corrupt a human being. This individual was a well-established person, a great writer and lecturer, and had many students all over the world. And how much money was at stake here? Just a few hundred dollars. Yet this trivial matter was of such urgency to this man that it filled his mind at a moment when the thoughts of a balanced person would be on higher matters.

Greed is the mother of all miseries. It is born of desire. The fear of being unable to obtain the objects of one's desire and the fear of losing the desirable objects already in hand create the conditions out of which greed arises. All great traditions of the world have their origins in revealed knowledge. The founding masters of those traditions were personally committed to austerity, inner purification, and selfless service. Theirs were lives of self-sacrifice. They were living examples of what they taught. But sadly, such sublime traditions soon become contaminated by greed. The flame of the pyre that consumed the body of my living guide reminded me that you don't necessarily become great just because you have an enlightened master. To become great you must renounce your trivial self. To do that, you have to be vigilant in thought, speech, and action. Be observant. Assess your strengths and weaknesses. Search for time-tested techniques to initiate the process of inner purification. And do not expect that just because you are the follower of a great tradition everything will automatically be great. Any authentic spiritual path requires self-transformation.

The Prince and the Dog

Two weeks after Swamiji's death, I traveled to Kanpur to visit one of his most beloved students, Dr. Sunanda Bai. She was one of the wisest and kindest people I have ever met. In the course of conversation, I shared my feelings about what had transpired after Swamiji died. She simply laughed and told me the following story:

Persian kings were known for building beautiful palaces. You know the special kind of palace known as *shish mahal,* the palace made of mirrors? Once a king built such a palace for his crown prince. It was fully furnished but the prince had not yet moved in as the final touches were still being applied.

One evening, right before the gate was closed, a dog wandered into the empty palace. Suddenly he noticed his reflection and was bewildered at seeing another dog. When he barked, the sound bounced back from every direction. Further bewildered, he looked all around and saw dogs everywhere. Now he was frightened. He ran back and forth barking at the other dogs, but the more he barked, the more they barked. When he jumped at one of the dogs, all the dogs jumped at him. Then he attacked one of the dogs with so much force that his mouth collided with a mirror, hurting his nose. He began to bleed. It was painful but suddenly he noticed that the other dogs were bleeding, too. He was filled with joy for he had discovered how to rip those other dogs apart. He began barking at himself and biting his own body. The joy of seeing the other dogs bleeding overshadowed his own pain. In the morning, when the caretakers entered the palace, they found the dog's body lying in a pool of blood. They dragged the corpse out and threw it on a rubbish heap far from the palace, cleaned up the blood, and prepared the room for the prince's visit.

Later that day, the prince and his retinue entered the palace. He admired every bit of it—the motifs, the tiles, the paintings. He praised the architects and the builders and distributed prizes to all those who had rendered their services. Finally he entered a chamber where mirrors were placed in a particularly intricate fashion. There he saw his reflection multiplied a hundred times. He stood in front of one of the mirrors, adjusted his mustache, stroked his beard, and gave himself a priceless smile. Immensely pleased, he ordered his treasurer to open the door of the treasury to those who had put so much of themselves into building this beautiful palace.

Both the dog and the prince entered the same palace, but each saw it differently. Why is that? The dog lacked self-understanding. He did not know that the other dogs in the mirror were his own reflection. Not wanting to share the palace with other dogs, he treated his own reflections as enemies. The prince knew who he was and he knew that the images appearing on the surface of the mirrors were his own reflections. He knew that those reflections were not claiming his palace. He enjoyed seeing his clear reflections and was amused by those which were somewhat distorted.

After telling me this story, the great lady, Dr. Sunanda Bai, remarked, "For a self-realized person, this world is like a beautiful palace, fitted with all the amenities. A self-realized soul lives in this world like a crown prince. He is neither the source of fear to others nor are others a source of fear to him. Dog-like creatures, lacking self-understanding, fight with others. They live in fear, they transmit their fear to others, and they die in fear."

Dr. Sunanda Bai

Sacred Link:
The Quest for Freedom

After my master died, living in India became unbearable for me. For the past twenty years, he had infused my heart with an inexhaustible wealth of love, leaving no room for any form of craving, and yet now, at the human level, I did not know how to fill the emotional gap created by his departure from this world. My discomfort was further compounded by the fact that a number of Swamiji's disciples were trying to drag me into a situation that I found trivial and meaningless—they were putting pressure on me to join them in their agenda to secure power and position in Swamiji's organization in India. To avoid this mess, I left India as quickly as I could. I reached the Institute's headquarters in Pennsylvania in the first week of December, just three weeks after my master's death.

For the next several months, a stream of people visited me daily, expressing a variety of thoughts, feelings, and sentiments. Some came to offer their condolences; others offered their love and support both for Swamiji's mission and for me. And others wanted me to remove their confusion by clarifying who was really Swamiji's successor. By this time, in India, in the United States, and in other parts of the world, a score of people were claiming to embody the wisdom of the sages passed on to them by Swamiji directly. Some were demanding that Swamiji's followers and "regular" students acknowledge them as his successor. The "evidence" produced by these "successors" was being circulated through word of mouth as well as by mass mailings. Furthermore, dozens of swamis suddenly came out of the cupboard, all sharing a similar story: Swamiji had conferred the highest level of initiation on them and had ordained them into the monastic order of the Himalayan sages. Each of them, at one time or another, demanded that I arrange a meeting with him where he and I, as the leading disciples of Swamiji, would decide and determine democratically the future shape and scope of Swamiji's spiritual work and mission. Proclaiming their loyalty to Swamiji, some of them went so far as to divorce their spouses, become renunciates, and start new organizations, claiming Swamiji, who was already deceased, as the founding spiritual head—only to fight among themselves later, shut down their organizations, and lose their entire life savings in the process.

While all of this was going on in the States, one of Swamiji's most senior students in India went on a hunger strike, threatening to starve himself to death unless he was given complete decision-making powers in all spiritual matters and was treated as the highest spiritual authority of "Swamiji's original spiritual seat" in Rishikesh. This he did with international-scale publicity, while local newspapers published his story with journalistic savor. Some people sent me the newspaper clippings and others sent faxes expressing their mixed feelings. Just looking at these clippings and faxes made me feel like throwing up.

Overcome with disgust, I handed over this correspondence to the president of the Institute and I went to my familiar refuge, Swamiji's loft. There I slipped into a state of reverie: Who is this master? What did he have? Who are we and what did we inherit from him? He was the son of a learned pandit. He became an orphan while still a young child. He was discarded by his own brother and looked after by a saint who owned nothing. Still, he managed to go to school, find time for spiritual practices, cultivate self-respect, conquer adverse conditions, and prove that through persistent practice, one can become perfect. In his early years, he was a hermit who spent his nights meditating in the Himalayan caves. In those days, he owned nothing except a loincloth and a water pot. Villagers came to him with milk and food, seeking nothing other than the unspoken name of God that naturally filled the space around him. When he came to the West, his role in the external world changed. He worked hard writing books, giving lectures, and administering a multinational charitable organization, and as such, he looked like a corporate CEO. But at midnight, he removed his worldly mask and assumed his true identity: the sleepless envoy of the Himalayan sages.

I kept reflecting: I lived with this master for twenty years. I had the opportunity to observe him closely and had found his life an open book with a clear message: Once you offer yourself to the Almighty Lord, the world naturally prostrates at your feet. Once you conquer your mind, you have conquered the world. Once you have found joy and beauty within, the whole world becomes infused with joy and beauty. Once you are successful inside, external success is yours. Once you surrender your desires to the Almighty, you are free of your personal whims and ambitions. The divine will itself becomes your desire.

Here we are, his students, I reflected, the disciples of the sage who during an outburst of ecstasy once sang:

Child am I of a sage of the mountain.
Free spirit am I; light walks by my side.
Fearless live I about glacial fountain,
In seclusion of Himalayan cavern reside.

With snowy weather beating around me,
Ascending the peaks of the mountains I go.
No one talks with me, no one walks with me,
As I cross streams and tramp glacial snow.

I roam in the mountains that hark to the skies,
And of silence have made me a friend.
My Love whispers to me with silent replies.
And guided by Thee I ascend.

Thoughts kept pouring in: Swamiji was an accomplished yogi with perfect mastery over his body, breath, and mind. How perfect was his posture. His legs would rise in the air and arrange themselves in the lotus pose; there he would sit for hours without the slightest movement. While sipping his chai, he would play with his brain, producing any band of brain wave—alpha, theta, beta or delta—at will. He could stop his heart by accelerating atrial fluttering, and he could shatter bulletproof glass by gazing at it from a twenty-foot distance. How many of us have learned any of these skills, which he used to call "yoga tricks"?

He was master of *yoga nidra,* through which he was able to provide, in a matter of thirty minutes, a more profound rest to his body and nervous system than one could get from an entire night's sleep. How many of us have really learned and mastered this art? With his limitless appetite for learning, he traveled from cave to cave, from monastery to monastery, and ultimately learned from his grandmaster in Tibet the science of *parakaya pravesh* (leaving the body voluntarily and entering the same or another body later at will), a *kriya* he demonstrated in strict laboratory conditions more than once. I wondered, how many of us have inherited this science or have even made an attempt to learn about it? Students are trying to succeed him—*in what?* What is this craving for claiming one's right, especially when we do not know what there is to be claimed?

While reflecting on all this, I was flooded by a memory of being with Swamiji. One day, years ago I walked into this very same loft. As I approached him, I saw his eyes were fixed on a book. Fifteen minutes later, he murmured, "When did you come?"

I answered, "Just a little while ago. What are you reading, Swamiji?"

He answered, "Tagore."

After a few minutes of silence, he said, "What a great soul he was. Like a breeze, such souls come to this world and live among humans, and yet rarely does anyone notice them."

Then, handing me the book, he said, "How profound is his wisdom." He put his finger on a sentence that read, "Man does not acquire rights through occupation of larger space, nor through external conduct, but his rights extend only so far as he is real, and his reality is measured by the scope of his consciousness."

Recollecting this encounter with Swamiji and the prolonged discussion that had transpired afterward led me to measure my own reality. I surveyed the present landscape of my consciousness and compared it with the past landscape. My self-assessment took me to my childhood. There, I saw myself growing up in a tiny north Indian village at a time when the entire country was embroiled in turmoil. As a child and adolescent, I saw the members of the upper castes feeding on sheer vanity while the members of the lower castes nourished themselves on vengeance. Mahatma Gandhi's efforts to infuse Hindu society with a sense of equality and equanimity had gone in vain. The gap between the upper and lower castes widened as each group tried to pull the other down. Hatred between Hindus and Muslims intensified as political and religious leaders exploited the anger of both groups for their own purposes. In the newly won democracy, while its leaders were still trying to figure out which particular economic and social system—capitalism, socialism, or communism—was best for India, the fabric of society was being strained by differences in ethnicity, language, caste, race, and sectarian belief. Wherever I looked, I saw fear, anger, and hatred arising from a sense of separation, alienation, and isolation. I saw politicians exploiting the poverty and ignorance that pervaded Indian society; I saw Muslims annoying Hindus by blasting their prayers from loudspeakers, and Hindus ridiculing Muslims with the taunt that their God was deaf.

It is in that India that I was born into a family steeped in the utter orthodoxy of Hinduism. They embraced their time-honored values with complete faith and reverence and yet respected others with a clear understanding that no one garment fits all. Today, I realize why my parents were so dearly loved by Hindus and Muslims, poor and rich, members of lower and upper castes alike. In those days, what was my understanding of life? What was the shape and size of my personal reality? What was the scope of my consciousness? Then I was too young to even consider these queries, but the trail of the incidences and circumstances of my past still preserved in my memory tells me that the Divine Providence, in its own mysterious ways, was always stretching the field of my consciousness, enabling me to comprehend an ever-expanding light of reality.

There was a time when I needed a god to protect me from ghosts who lived in dust devils, but the scope of my consciousness in those days was such that it could accommodate a god only the size of an onion. As the level of my comprehension increased, Hanuman, a god embodying greater power and wisdom, made his residence in my heart. His company granted me greater security, higher protection, and a level of freedom from fear greater than I had ever known. Yet, there was a gap between that god and me. He extended his help only when I asked. He heard my prayers only when I recited them. There was a need-based relationship between the two of us. Clearly, my love for God was conditional and my faith in him was experimental.

Then one day, the Lord of Life, the center of all mysteries, lifted another layer of the veil covering my soul, giving me, for the first time, a taste of unconditional love. This time, she used my distant uncles to bring me closer to her bosom. When they threw me in the compost pit in an attempt to finish me off, she was there to protect me even before I sought her help. From this experience came the unshakable conviction that God resides not only in temples and churches, holy scriptures and sacred prayers, but even in a compost pit. I realized that his loving and protecting arms stretch in every direction. There is no place where these mighty arms can't reach. The Lord of Life is not a merchant who trades prayers for protection. This Lord is the director of everyone's performance. With his masterful maneuvering, even a most dreadful deed can serve as a springboard for jumping high in the sky of Divine Providence and landing where everything is good and auspicious. After this experience I was overcome by a craving to see this Living Reality face-to-face. The direct experience of her unconditional love had convinced me that she is not an abstract idea.

Now I wanted to know more about her and her relationship to me, so as to adore her in a manner that befits her splendor. For years, I worked hard with my self-proclaimed sincerity without the slightest idea that my yearning to know her was incomplete and fragmented. Then one day, grace descended, and I got a glimpse of the bitter reality: I was lost in the midst of my own desires.

It happened in 1976 when I was 23 years old. I had just completed my master's degree and was enrolled in a

Swami Rama during his last days

Ph.D. program. I was actively looking for a job—a job that could bring me name, fame, honor, money, and prestige. Yet the inner calling of my soul was demanding whether I was really interested in those worldly achievements. Fear and anxiety had me in their grip. I was being ground between the two stones of wanting and not-wanting. Never before had I experienced this kind of restlessness. This is when I met my master, Swami Rama, who, with his magic touch, lifted the veil of my confusion, enabling me to comprehend the unfathomable grandeur of the Soul of the Universe, who, through her sheer will, contracts her glory so that she may reside in our hearts without overwhelming our souls. At the wake of this experience, I was struck with wonder—how amazing! He is in me. He *is* me. He is in the universe. He *is* the universe. To know and to be with this Great One, all I have to do is let the little things go. I realized how blindly I was running after charms and temptations of the world, and how the more I hankered after worldly success, the poorer I had become. Instantly, my tears of gratitude fell at his feet, for I couldn't contain the thrill that the light I was seeking was sitting before me in the flesh. The quest for freedom was now at hand. The question of whether truth is within or without, manifest or unmanifest, far or near, had lost its meaning.

Living for twenty years in the sheltered environment of the Himalayan Institute, I had lost sight of the reality most people have. I had forgotten the conflicts and complications that beset people when I was growing up in the village. I no longer remembered how disgusted I had been during my college years seeing the misery caused by lust for money, power, prestige, and self-aggrandizement. Now once again, this reality had come back around. This time, Swamiji's own students, my friends who at some point had been near to me, were stirring up unrest and upsetting the balance of a peaceful community. For a while, I was disturbed and sad, for it was hitting me directly in the face. My patience and inner stability were put to the test. I am thankful to the inner guide who took me to Swamiji's loft and pushed me into a contemplative state where I found my master reading the work of one of his own teachers, Rabindranath Tagore. This contemplation made me revisit my past and comprehend the cause not only of the disturbance among Swamiji's students but also of fear and violence, anger and hatred, and vengeance in our families, schools, streets, and communities worldwide.

The intense and self-absorbing contemplation that I returned to again and again after my master's passing one day pushed me into that corner of my memory that held the solution to the strife that is gripping humanity so tightly today. Just a few days after our first meeting, I had asked Swamiji about the cause of the fear and anxiety that had taken over my life after I graduated from college. His answer was brief and compact:

"It is your desires, the legitimacy of which you never examined. Desires are very subtle. Their very presence contaminates the purity of your faith in yourself and the Divine. Their very presence clouds your mind from seeing the difference between the divine will and your personal whims, the call of your soul and the deceptive agenda of your mind. The inner unrest caused by subtle desires forces the mind to find a justification, but divine grace overrides all this melodrama. Don't you remember when she lovingly slapped you on the cheek and told you, 'I know better than you about you. I am your life. . . .'? All of your confusion, fear, and anxiety vanished instantly. You were back to your normal self, charged with the conviction that on the quest for freedom, she is with you."

Then Swamiji shared with me the distillation of the message of the sages:

"You are an eternal traveler. From time immemorial, you have been marching toward the fullest realization of your soul—your core being, the center of consciousness. This consciousness is greater than all the objects, thoughts, and ideas you can ever accumulate and conjure. It is greater than all of your deeds, glorious and disgraceful combined. Neither the outward expression nor inward repose of this consciousness can be touched by death, decay, or destruction. Don't identify yourself with the petty details of your life. As a spiritual seeker, however, if you reflect on them with purpose, then those petty details will reveal a great wisdom—they have been a prelude to the final realization of your soul. At the dawn of this revelation, your thoughts, speech, and actions unite themselves in an inner harmony.

"You are then led to the next level of realization—the Lord of Life residing in your heart and in the hearts of all living beings is the ultimate center of everything that is. She is the heart of your heart and the soul of your soul. This realization spares no room for anyone outside you— temples and mosques, counselors and clergy—to define your being, for you know your relationship with yourself and with the only one Absolute Divine who shines in the hearts of all living beings. This realization frees you from your addiction to self-gratification, insatiable greed, and pride of possession, and grants you freedom from the pain and strife caused by the insolent alienation of the heart. Without this realization, you will have neither the motivation nor courage to give up your trivial self and see truth face-to-face. Failure to face your own reality will force you to live in vain only to be met by the stiffening shroud of death over and over again."

Seven years ago my master left his body. Since then, my travels have taken me all over the world. I have met people from all walks of life—poor and rich, old and young, illiterate and educated. By and large, all I saw was separation and strife. Despite the valiant efforts of thousands of organizations, both government and private, the gap between the poor and the rich is widening. High-minded groups such as the United Nations and the World Parliament of Religions hold frequent peace summits, and yet political and religious war is as pervasive as ever. Despite great advances in human rights, the condition of women in many parts of the world remains deplorable. Then consider poverty and all the ills that go with it: the continuing assault on the environment, the exploitation of children, the extinction of tribal peoples—the list goes on. Turn your attention to the countries blessed with material prosperity. There you see misery in other forms: high divorce rates, domestic violence, children suffering from depression, and the growing incidence of stress-related diseases. What is the cause of all this misery? Tagore explains it beautifully:

> Man can destroy and plunder, earn and accumulate, invent and discover, but he is great because his soul comprehends all. It is dire destruction for him when he envelops his soul in a dead shell of callous habits, and when a blind fury of works whirls around him like an eddying dust storm, shutting out the horizon. That indeed kills the very spirit of his being which is the spirit of comprehension. . . . By this power of comprehension, this permeation of his being, he is united with the all-pervading spirit. . . . Where a man tries to raise himself to eminence by pushing and jostling all others, to

achieve a distinction by which he prides himself to be more than everybody else, there he is alienated from that spirit.

Later, commenting on a passage from the New Testament, Tagore writes, "Whatever we treasure for ourselves separates us from others; our possessions are our limitations. He who is bent upon accumulating riches is unable, with his ego continually bulging, to pass through the gates of comprehension of the spiritual world, which is the world of perfect harmony; he is shut up within the narrow walls of his limited acquisitions."

It is my conviction that the wisdom that my master gathered from previous sages can save the spirit of the human race; the wisdom without which human beings will have no choice but to continue eating their own flesh with the deluded hope of freeing themselves from their perpetual hunger. It is this gift of understanding that I have received as an inheritance. It is this wisdom my master, the sage of the Himalayas, left for everyone.

Today, I wish to share the love that I received from this great soul, but I cannot, for I am still a child. Maturity of expression escapes me. My heart is open, but my lips are sealed. All I can do is share my prayer; perhaps that will suffice to make up for my shortcomings:

I am your lamp. "My" flame is yours. Thank you, Gurudeva, my master, for infusing my heart with your grace—the realization that it is your love that gives me strength and insight to surrender all that I am to the light. Who could be kind like you, who, without weighing my merits and demerits, took me to the Lord of Life and placing me at her feet urged, "Here is your child in dire need of your nurturing glance. Please manifest yourself in him."

Thus was lit the flame of Sacred Link.

In the light of this flame I saw a world where great and small meet in mutual respect; where gain and loss surrender their holdings; and where losers pray for winners' peace, and the shamefaced winners relinquish their spoils to those they defeated. Today, as a humble offering to the heart of hearts and soul of souls, I recast my prayers:

> May this Light walk by my side, enlightening all so they may know that freedom from fear is the cornerstone of peace, and that peace is the ground for happiness. May this Light help people understand that alienation is the cause of inner unrest; that this alienation arises when we experience ourselves as isolated beings. May I go on tirelessly carrying this lamp of Sacred Link door-to-door, heart-to-heart—from nation to nation, culture to culture. I know very well that this is how I will complete my own quest, for I am an extension of your masterful work. For as long as you wish, my Master, go on filling this lamp with oil to keep the flame high and bright. Following your will, I join you in your eternal abode, Mount Kailash.

About *the* Author

Pandit Rajmani Tigunait, Ph.D., the spiritual head of the Himalayan Institute®, is the successor of Swami Rama of the Himalayas. Lecturing and teaching worldwide for more than a quarter of a century, he is a regular contributor to *Yoga International* magazine and the author of twelve books, including the best-selling *At the Eleventh Hour: The Biography of Swami Rama of the Himalayas.*

Pandit Tigunait holds two doctorates: one in Sanskrit from the University of Allahabad in India and another in Oriental Studies from the University of Pennsylvania. Family tradition gave Pandit Tigunait access to a vast range of spiritual wisdom preserved in both the written and oral traditions. Before meeting his master, Swami Rama, Pandit Tigunait studied Sanskrit, the language of the ancient scriptures of India, as well as the languages of the Buddhist, Jain, and Zoroastrian traditions. In 1976, Swami Rama ordained Pandit Tigunait into the 5,000-year-old lineage of the Himalayan masters.

the Himalayan Institute

The main building of the Institute headquarters, near Honesdale, Pennsylvania.

Founded in 1971 by Swami Rama, the Himalayan Institute has been dedicated to helping people grow physically, mentally, and spiritually by combining the best knowledge of both the East and the West.

Our international headquarters is located on a beautiful 400-acre campus in the rolling hills of the Pocono Mountains of northeastern Pennsylvania. The atmosphere here is one to foster growth, increased inner awareness, and calm. Our grounds provide a wonderfully peaceful and healthy setting for our seminars and extended programs. Students from all over the world join us here to attend programs in such diverse areas as hatha yoga, meditation, stress reduction, Ayurveda, nutrition, Eastern philosophy, psychology, and other subjects. Whether the programs are for weekend meditation retreats, week-long seminars on spirituality, months-long residential programs, or holistic health services, the attempt here is to provide an environment of gentle inner progress. We invite you to join with us in the ongoing process of personal growth and development.

The Institute is a nonprofit organization. Your membership in the Institute helps to support its programs. Please call or write for information on becoming a member.

Programs and Services *include:*

- Weekend or extended seminars and workshops
- Meditation retreats and advanced meditation instruction
- Hatha yoga teachers' training
- Residential programs for self-development
- Holistic health services and pancha karma at the Institute's Center for Health and Healing
- Spiritual excursions
- Varcho Veda® herbal products
- Himalayan Institute Press
- *Yoga International* magazine
- Sanskrit correspondence course

A Quarterly Guide to Programs and Other Offerings is free within the USA. To request a copy, or for further information, call 800-822-4547 or 570-253-5551, write to the Himalayan Institute, 952 Bethany Turnpike, Building 1, Honesdale, PA 18431, USA, or visit our website at www.HimalayanInstitute.org

HIMALAYAN INSTITUTE®

P R E S S

Himalayan Institute Press has long been regarded as "The Resource for Holistic Living." We publish dozens of titles, as well as audio and video tapes that offer practical methods for living harmoniously and achieving inner balance. Our approach addresses the whole person—body, mind, and spirit—integrating the latest scientific knowledge with ancient healing and self-development techniques.

As such, we offer a wide array of titles on physical and psychological health and well-being, spiritual growth through meditation and other yogic practices, as well as translations of yogic scriptures.

Our yoga accessories include the Japa Kit for meditation practice and the Neti Pot™, the ideal tool for sinus and allergy sufferers. Our Varcho Veda® line of quality herbal extracts is now available to enhance balanced health and well-being.

Subscriptions are available to a bimonthly magazine, *Yoga International,* which offers thought-provoking articles on all aspects of meditation and yoga, including yoga's sister science, Ayurveda.

For a free catalog, call 800-822-4547 or 570-253-5551, email hibooks@HimalayanInstitute.org, fax 570-647-1552, write to Himalayan Institute Press, 630 Main St., Suite 350, Honesdale, PA 18431-1843, USA, or visit our website at www.HimalayanInstitute.org

A Preview of

Prophecies
of the Sages
The Destiny of Mankind

An upcoming book by
PANDIT RAJMANI TIGUNAIT, PH.D.

I am recasting a prophecy that my master made at the eve of his life; a prophecy that masters in the East have made more than once; a prophecy that the earth beneath our feet is telling us loudly and clearly even today . . . It is a prophecy that explains why the earth is becoming increasingly barren, flowers are losing their aroma, fruits are becoming tasteless, and humans of both sexes are becoming infertile. This prophecy is not as much about the extinction of the human race or life on the planet as it is a clear warning about a rich and diverse civilization—our civilization—coming to an abrupt end, and leaving us in a Dark Age to start all over again. Today I share with you when and how I came to know about these predictions, and what exactly compelled me to talk about them with a world which normally pays attention to warnings only after a preventable catastrophe has run its course.

Every age and culture has its prophets and its forecasts, most of which concern cataclysms—war, pestilence, earthquakes, tidal waves, and a host of other natural disasters. *Exactly where and when they will occur and the scope of the devastation are usually matters of interpretation and dispute, but the prophecies provoke terror in spite of the fact that often they do not come to pass. For example, in the past, prophets and other visionaries warned us that the world would end 1,400 years after the inception of Islam (a date which fell in the 1980s); now they are telling us that California and New York City will soon drop into the sea. Those who predict such calamities never tell us how we can avert them, or prepare ourselves to face them, because they assume that these events are predestined.*

The prophecies made by the sages in the East are a breed apart. Rather than confining themselves to predicting calamities, the sages focus on the basic characteristics of human existence— our strength, intelligence, capacity, spiritual development, material wealth, longevity, harmony with nature, connection with divine forces, and so on. The sages explain why catastrophes happen and what we can do to forestall them. They are not as much interested in prophesying calamitous events as they are in telling us how to transform them through our individual and collective efforts.

These passages are excerpts from an upcoming book from Pandit Rajmani Tigunait, Ph.D., author of Touched by Fire. Slated for publication in September 2005, this enlightening book explores the likelihood, based on the prophecies of Eastern sages, that humankind is currently in the midst of Kali Yuga, the cycle of the dark age.

"It is a prophecy that concerns the destiny of the human race and the fate of our planet," writes Tigunait. "It is a prophecy that forecasts the outcome of the war between the forces of darkness and light. It is about the outcome of the clash or commingling of science and spirituality."

Of course, we all want reassurance that light will prevail and the unrest that causes so much violence, suffering, and injustice will come to an end. No less human than the rest of us, Tigunait seemed to seek the same from his master in one recounted conversation, held in the early 1990s. But Swami Rama simply explained that, unless we can overcome the fear that grips human minds and hearts, we will enter a time of terrible trial.

"Despite our mastery of the external world, we are run by fear. We need a politician to grant us homeland security, religious leaders to grant us spiritual security, therapists to grant us psychological security, police to make us feel safe on the streets, physicians and specialists to secure our physical health, lawyers to secure our rights, and insurance companies to rescue us when all these protections fail," Swami Rama said to Tigunait. "What people are not realizing is that fear invites danger. As long as we keep postponing the basic problem, that is, overcoming fear itself, we will continue creating wars within and without. We'll fight at home; we'll fight on the streets. Hindus will fight with Muslims; Easterners will fight with Westerners. Fear is the raw material that the mind uses to manufacture enemies. Once the enemy is manufactured, it must reach the market. It is a simple and invariable law."

Spurred on by these conversations with his master, Tigunait thoroughly explores the prophecies that have been foretold for centuries about the cycle of the dark age that we have, undoubtedly, already entered. It is thought-provoking and often frightening material. But he does not leave us without hope. "If we follow the path of *dharma*—the perennial law of nature—and if we grease our thoughts, speech, and actions with love, compassion, and respect for all, we can definitely turn the wheel around, transforming the dark age into the golden one," he writes.

Prophecies of the Sages explains that only by relearning the truth that nothing in creation exists apart from anything else, by actually embracing the principles at the heart of our religions (which most practitioners currently ignore), and by learning to see the Divine in everyone and everything around us, we can restore peace and happiness on earth. Such a feat, of course, must be accomplished on an individual basis, one person at a time. That's why Tigunait charges the reader to discover the Sacred Link™ between your core self and the endless layers of reality within and without.

"This will enable you to see and bask in a beauty beyond the fleeting standards imposed by the fashion industry," he writes. "It will transport you to a world of joy far more profound than the pleasures offered by the entertainment industry. Discovering the Sacred Link™ within yourself will enable you to hear the pulsation of endless hearts in your soul; it will take you to a new level of sensitivity to your own feelings and the feelings of others. This discovery will charge your mind with decisiveness and your speech and actions with purpose and meaning."

FOR MORE INFORMATION ABOUT . . .

visit our
website

www.HimalayanInstitute.org